RAIN DELAYS

RAIN DELAYS

Bert Randolph Sugar

With a Foreword by Joe Garagiola

St. Martin's Press / New York

Design by Richard Oriolo

Library of Congress Cataloging-in-Publication Data

Sugar, Bert Randolph.
    Rain delays : the anecdotal history of baseball / Bert Randolph
Sugar.
        p. cm.
    "A Thomas Dunne Book."
    ISBN 0-312-04411-9
    1. Baseball—United States—History—Miscellanea. 2. Baseball—
United States—Anecdotes. I. Title.
GV873.S89   1990
796.357'0973—dc20   89-77645
                                                    CIP

First Edition
10 9 8 7 6 5 4 3 2 1

This book is lovingly dedicated to
Red Smith and Dick Young,
two writer-raconteurs who kept
the flame alive with their
storytelling and whose
ample echoes are
with us still.

Contents

Foreword

*R*ain Delays is a wonderful title for a book of anecdotes, because at a ballpark when there's a rain delay, the stories start being told. That's true in the broadcasting booth, in the dugout, in the clubhouse, in the press box, or wherever people are sitting around waiting for the rain to stop.

Even in the bull pen—providing it has a cover—you can hear some wild things during a rain delay. I was on a club with a relief pitcher, Dick Hall, who had been a Phi Beta Kappa quality student in college. During a rain delay, he took out a pencil and paper (this was before calculators), and a watch, and figured out how much water was falling on the field.

In the broadcast booth, there are some guys who hate rain delays. A broadcaster has to scoot around looking for somebody he can interview, or turn himself into an instant weatherman, or just tell stories. Rainouts never bothered me at the ballpark. Playing was what gave me problems. Talking about baseball and the people in it was always something I enjoyed.

I happen to believe that books like this one, which deal with the stories, true and untrue, that baseball people tell, are a must for fans. I think baseball has more and funnier anecdotes than any other sport.

Funny things happen on ball fields. (Russ Meyer once got so mad at an umpire's decision on a pitch that he threw the rosin bag straight up in the air, put both hands on his hips, and stood on the mound glaring at the umpire. The rosin bag came down right on top of his head.)

Funny things are said on ball fields. (When Seattle manager, Joe Schultz, came out to get pitcher Fred Talbot, instead of arguing Talbot said, "Where in the world have you been? I thought you'd never get here.")

Funny things are said in broadcast booths, and not always on purpose. (After Phil Rizzuto complimented a shortstop for catching a pop fly, even though the left fielder was bearing down on him, Phil's broadcast partner, Billy Martin, said, "You hear those footprints, don't you?")

The truth is that the things that have been said about baseball over the years, the ones I remember, anyway, have been not just about baseball, but about subjects like dining, music, religion, politics, eclipses, history, youth fitness, and self-protection, just to name a few. Here are some examples:

Dining? Willie Stargell's comment on a game when Steve Carlton was at the top of his form in beating the Pirates: "Hitting at him tonight was like to trying to eat soup with a fork."

Music? In Shea Stadium one night, Pirates pitcher, Nellie Briles, sang the "Star-Spangled Banner." At the conclusion of the anthem, Pittsburgh baseball writer Charley Feeney told the people in the press box, "Briles is the first Pittsburgh pitcher to finish since August twenty-third."

Religion? For that we turn to the man who made the phrase, "Don't look back, something might be gaining on you." part of the American language. It was Leroy "Satchel" Paige, who also said, "Don't pray when it rains, if you don't pray when the sun shines."

Politics? A master politician once gave a masterful political answer when asked to pick a World Series winner. Said vice president Hubert Humphrey, "I take a national view of the American League, and an American view of the National League."

Eclipses? Sure. It was 1970 when Pittsburgh general manager Joe Brown wrote to John Quinn, the Phillies general manager asking for a one-hour delay in the start of an exhibition game because of a scheduled total eclipse of the sun. He added, "It may interest you to know that the next eclipse in our hemisphere will be on April eighth, 2024. Let's try to schedule around it."

History? Well, that came from a baseball executive, too. Bill DeWitt once showed what the baseball brass thinks about after they leave the game. He said, "The bathtub was invented in 1850. The telephone was invented in 1875. Do you realize what that means? It means that if you had been living in 1850, you could have sat in the bathtub for twenty-five years without having to get up to answer the telephone."

Youth fitness? There has long been a question of just how much physical well-being is helped by playing baseball. James White, a physical education professor at the University of California—San Diego, had a theory as to its value to young- sters. Professor White said, "The only real exercise Little

League affords is the two-hundred-yard sprint to the snack stand after the game."

Under the heading of self-protection comes a quote that has to rank as one of the real "zingers" one player ever laid on another. After Milwaukee pitcher, Jim Colborn, hit Aurelio Rodriguez with a pitch, he later heard that Rodriguez had threatened to break a bat over his head. Said Colburn, "All I'd have to do is make my head look like a slider, and he'd miss it."

One year I was doing the World Series pre-game show in Oakland. Just as I was signing off, I said, "One advantage in being bald is that you know it's raining before everyone else. Right now, I have to tell you, 'Raindrops Are Falling On My Head.' " Turned out there was no game that night. It was called off after a one hour . . . that's right . . . rain delay.

Speaking of rain delays, why don't you turn the page and see what Bert Sugar has for you in the way of "Rain Delays." I'm sure you'll enjoy it. I did.

—JOE GARAGIOLA
Scottsdale, Arizona
February 16, 1990

Joe Garagiola has been part of the major league baseball scene since he broke in as a catcher for his hometown St. Louis Cardinals in 1946. Still an active baseball broadcaster, Joe is also the president of the Baseball Assistance Team (BAT), a group of former major league players dedicated to helping the less fortunate members of the baseball family who missed out on the seven-figure salaries and big pensions. Tax deductible contributions may be sent to BAT, 350 Park Avenue, New York, NY 10022, with the knowledge that *Every Single Penny* will go to help some former baseball person.

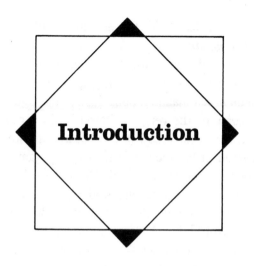

Introduction

This collection of stories and anecdotes had its origins in the 1977 World Series. Not through something that happened down on the field, but through something that happened off the field.

Before the third game of the Series I found myself standing around the Yankees' hospitality suite looking as bereft as Robinson Crusoe without a boat, practicing servilities and other obsequities, when Dick Schaap approached and asked me to "look out" for a gentleman he had in tow. The gentleman, an elderly man with a care-ploughed face punctuated with a faint impersonal smile that seemed to cover something of contempt, was introduced as Jim Farrell. Truth to tell, this was no plain ol' Jim Farrell, but the hero of my adolescence, James T. Farrell, author of my youthful bible, *Studs Lonigan.*

As a gnarled hand, which looked as if it had been trampled on, was extended in my general direction, the opening lines of his magnum opus flashed through my mind: "Studs Lonigan, on the verge of fifteen, and wearing his first suit of long trousers, stood in the bathroom with a Sweet Caporal pasted in his mug. His hands were jammed in his trouser pockets, and he sneered. He puffed, drew the fag out of his mouth, inhaled, and said to himself: Well, I'm kissin' the old dump good-bye tonight." But tonight the subject was baseball, baseball, and more baseball, and Farrell launched into several stories—stories that didn't stop at the three-mile limit, but continued beyond, ex post facto. First he told of how Bugs Baer, on the occasion of Smead Jolley going four-for-four, had written, "He had the greatest day since Lizzie Borden went two-for-two in Fall River, Massachusetts." Then he told of the "Black Sox" and their throwing the 1919 Series. And then he began to tell other stories, tracing the yellowing news clips in his memory like bread crumbs back to the antediluvian days of baseball.

Pretty soon we were joined by other storytellers, so many in fact that their talents were available at a discount. Deciding it was a bad bargain that couldn't run both ways, they joined in with other stories, mostly never-heard-before tales, not standard size-six stories. There were such great storytellers as Harold Rosenthal, Red Smith, Dick Young, Dan Daniel, Sam Taub, and others, all going that somewhere whither their lucky mounts might convey them in a stop-me-if-you've-heard-this-one-before manner. Nobody did.

The game was now about to begin, and the tiny knot of racounteurs repaired to their seats in the auxiliary press box. I, of course, took great care to make sure I not only accompanied this moveable feast, but sat down with them, right next to Jim Farrell. As the action on the field went on apace, the cracker-barrel huggers continued on their merry, the curriculum of their stories a wide one, seemingly without geographical boundaries. I remember Red Smith telling how he felt the first time he sat down between Grantland Rice and Ring Lardner and savored their inexhaustible hoard of stories. My own sensation was similar—it was a veritable smorgasbord for a young writer.

Farrell studied his cigarette the way a scientist might study a beetle, cupped his hand to catch the falling ashes, and continued to tell his tales—some a little airbrushed over, others told with more than a tinge of the white hue. The other fully paid-up members of the storytelling guild waited around like numbers at a meat market, knowing it was well to be done with the old story before they began the new. Some of the tales were repeating decimals—anyone keeping footnotes could have written *Ibid.*—while others were undiscovered treasures, dug up and dusted off after lo these many years. Bivouacked there at Farrell's crooked elbow, I witnessed an amazing regentrification—not only of the tale-tellers themselves, but of baseball as well—as the sports' hardened arteries turned into its lifeline to the past.

Suddenly those who had long ago learned to run when a grizzly began with "Once upon a time . . ." were collecting around, drawn as much by the timeless allure of good baseball stories as by the touch of genius and genuflection with which they were told. But Farrell greeted newcomers under forty with a stare that would have caused burnt toast to curl up around the edges. They were, Farrell hinted, the reason why baseball storytelling had fallen into disrepair. It was almost a case of baseball's version of Gresham's Law, the bad stories having forced the good ones out of circulation. And while he might forgive them for the same reason he could forgive Jack the Ripper—they were human, after all— he was not going to have these young dandruff-scratchers insert their oars in any storytelling session he was engaged in.

As the stories continued in heaping platefuls, I reflected on Farrell's unstated but strongly implied point. Surely this was not without meaning, I thought. Granted there were so few good baseball stories around that they seemed suspended like fruit in aspic. But was it the fault of the press?

Back in baseball's primordial days the world in a golden airship wafted on just two wings: print and stories. There were nine morning dailies and seven evenings in New York alone, and every writer worth his vital two-cent essay could fill a column to the Plimsoll line with stories, stories, and more stories. But starting in the 1920s the newspapers in New York and elsewhere began to dwindle to a precious few. Suddenly writers had to fight for space. And with each other. No longer could they immerse themselves in romantic and honorable devotion to stories. They now had to resort to facts, there being no need—nor room—to embroider. Beginning in the thirties, there was a general feeling that truth made all things plain. Then, starting in the forties and escalating in the fifties, came a school of journalism that could best be described as the I-say-it's-spinach-and-I-say-the-hell-with-it school. The stories, which had once come in generous potations, were now in disfavor, and those who told them were considered to have too much imagination to be honest.

Also in the fifties, television became a major medium, and with it the physiognomy of journalism changed forever.

Now it was headlines in fifteen-second bites. And talking-head announcers, who checked in and out of the spotlight like emperors in the wake of Nero, more renowned for their personalities than their performances. Their cumulative storytelling could be written on a postcard—with more than enough room left over for an address and an oversized postage stamp.

There are several theories about why storytelling is no longer a vital part of the baseball landscape. One theory, espoused by sportswriter-historian Red Foley, holds that modern-day conveniences are at fault. In days of old, players congregated in hotel lobbies because there was no air conditioning in rooms, and they whiled away the hours telling stories. Now the hotels are air-conditioned, with a TV set in each room, so the players no longer feel the need to sit in lobbies. Moreover, back then players had roomies, whereas now they have no one to share stories with. Furthermore, according to Foley, when players traveled on trains stories were the negotiable commodity between players and writers. Since today's team travels by plane, players can buckle up and go to sleep, and, except during the rare card games, talk to no one. In short, players today have only a nodding acquaintance with other players, let alone the writers covering the teams.

The other theory, given voice by Davey Jones, outfielder for the old, old Detroit Tigers, in Larry Ritter's excellent book *The Glory of Their Times,* holds, pure and simple, that "it was more *fun* to play ball then." That fun was expressed in stories and in nicknames—nicknames such as "the Georgia Peach," "the Sultan of Swat," "Dazzy," "Dizzy," "Daffy," "Ducky," and hundreds of others, some fanciful and some descriptive. Today's stars—such as George Brett, Wade

Boggs, Nolan Ryan, Don Mattingly, and an entire laundry list of names—go through their baseball lives without any sort of fun attached to their names. And agents, salaries, strikes, chemical substances, and other modern trappings of the game are hardly the stuff that stories are made of. Any stories that come out of these meager surroundings are merely skim milk masquerading as cream.

Small wonder then that storytelling has been left in the hands of those who haven't yet collapsed under the collective weight of their memories; who tell stories about olden times, fun times, and about players—not agents, salaries, strikes, or drugs. For, as Jim Farrell once said, "We American men are a nation of frustrated baseball players, and the literature of our childhood was morning-after stories. . . ."

Sure, some of those "morning-after stories" that date back to right after Father Adam first heard the apple alarm err on the side of storytelling rather than fact. Take, for instance, one of the most romantic stories ever to come down the baseball pike, of when, during the 1909 World Series, Ty Cobb supposedly stood on first and hollered down at Pittsburgh shortstop Honus Wagner, "Hey, Krauthead, I'm coming down on the next pitch!" Here Wagner would tell the rest of the story, usually trading his version for a growler of beer. "I told him to come ahead," one barkeep who heard Wagner tell the story several times remembers the Dutchman saying. "And by golly, he did," Wagner would go on. "But George Gibson, our catcher, laid the ball perfect, right in my glove, and I stuck it on Ty as he came in. I guess I wasn't too easy about it, 'cause it took three stiches to sew up his lip."

However, the incident "remembered" by Wagner for public consumption doesn't go down easily, but instead should be listed under those covered in the George Gershwin song "It Ain't Necessarily So." For in that 1909 Series between the Tigers and the Pirates, Cobb got on base nine times in twenty-nine at-bats. He tried to steal but three times, twice successfully—a theft of second in the first game and a theft of home in the second. The only time he failed must be marked with an asterisk, his attempt to steal second in game four resulting in a run-down that ended when first baseman Bill Abstein dropped the ball and allowed Cobb to take second unmolested. But Wagner, who had a well-deserved reputation for bellying up to the bar and recounting twice-told tales, continued to amuse his drinking cronies with his version of the play, a version picked up by dishonest ventriloquists and made part of baseball from that time forward. Still, it made one helluva story. Or a reasonable facsimile thereof.

And that's what this book is all about: baseball told through its stories even if, like the Wagnerian fairy tale, some of them can't stand up to the strictest investigation and can be called baseball history only in the sense that raisins can be called fruits: technically, and only in a manner of speaking.

In compiling this collection of stories and anecdotes I am indebted to the men who served as storytellers, leaving behind them genetic links to baseball's past. Men like Bob Addie, Lee Allen, Arthur "Bugs" Baer, Furman Bisher, Clifford Bloodgood, Bob Broeg, Heywood Broun, Warren Brown, Bozeman Bulger, Jimmy Cannon, John Carmichael, Bennett Cerf, Dave Condon, Bill Corum, Robert Creamer, Arthur Daley, Dan Daniel, John Drebinger, Chauncy Durden, Charlie Einstein, Red Foley, Peter Golenbock, Frank Graham, Milt Gross, Bill Heinz, Jerry Holtzman, Don Honig, Hype Igoe, Bill James, Roger Kahn, John Kieran, Ring Lardner, Fred Lieb, Bill Madden, Bill McGeehan, Tom Meany, Sid Mercer, Willard Mullin, Jim Murray, Barney Nagler, Dan Parker, Phil Pepe, Shirley Povich, Francis J. Powers, Grantland Rice, Larry Ritter, Harold Rosenthal, Irving Rudd, Damon Runyon, Dick Schaap, Al Silverman, Frank Slocum, H. Allen Smith, Ira Smith, Lyall Smith, Walter "Red" Smith, Robert Smith, Al Spink, J. G. Taylor Spink, John Steadman, Casey Stengel, J. Roy Stockton, Sam Taub, John Wheeler, Bill Veeck, and Dick Young.

And, of course, a special tip of the Sugar hat to Jim Farrell, who, unbeknownst to himself, inspired this goodly collection of good reads.

BERT RANDOLPH SUGAR
Chappaqua, New York
June 7, 1989

**RAIN
DELAYS**

The Early Years: Pre-1900 to 1910

Mike "King" Kelly was the post popular player in the early days of the national game, the man who came to be celebrated in the song "Slide, Kelly, Slide." King Kelly was the quickest thinker and the brainiest ballplayer in the early history of the game, inventing and perfecting plays that are now in the repertoire of every club. Rules were revised and rerevised to cover Kelly's antics, because every time one was written, Kelly would devise some new way of beating the system.

One winter the game's lawmakers changed the rules to permit managers to take players out of the game during play and substitute others. A few weeks after the season opened, the White Stockings were playing the Detroit Nationals—

called by some the Wolverines—with Kelly on the bench and the delightfully named Silver Flint catching for the Chicago nine. With the bases crowded to the gunnels with Detroiters and a safety meaning probable defeat for the defending champion White Stockings, the batter hit a high foul that neither Flint nor first baseman "Cap" Anson had a chance to reach. But Kelly, sitting on the bench, saw that he had a chance for the ball. Springing from the bench, Kelly shouted at the top of his voice, "Flint, you're out of the game," and then calmly caught the ball. But the umpire, named Gaffney (first name not known), refused to allow the catch, even when Kelly read the rule to him. The only result of Kelly's one-up-manship was that the following winter the rule was changed—again.

There's not a man still alive who can remember seeing Mike "King" Kelly play; alas, few remember him at all. But for years he lit up baseball's skies with fireworks, and when he was sold by the Chicago White Stockings to the Boston Red Stockings for $10,000 in 1887 he was called "the Ten Thousand Dollar Beauty." But even before that he was "the Great Kelly," what the fans—then called "Cranks"—in those quaint days called "a real beauty!"

Take the time the White Stockings were playing Detroit, with the score 2–2 in the ninth inning. Kelly got on first by beating out a bunt and big Ned Williamson drew a free pass off Detroit pitcher Stump Weidman. The two then engineered a double steal, but as Kelly slid into third he howled with pain and called for time.

Williamson rushed over to adminster to his teammate.

As he approached Kelly, the Great One said, "Ed, for the love of heaven, pull my arm. Faith, I think it's out of joint." Williamson proceeded to pull, and as he did so, Kelly whispered to him from under his mustache, "Say, Ed, soon as Weidman raises his arm I'm going to make a break for home. You sneak along behind, see. They'll play for me, sure, and forget about you. But when I'm close, I'll straddle my legs, and you slide under."

Kelly then returned to third, still writhing, so the spectators thought, in pain; Williamson resumed his position at second. In a second Kelly was roaring down the base path, and even Weidman was fooled by the miraculous recovery of the injured player. Kelly closed to within ten feet of home plate before Weidman, still unbelieving, threw the ball to Detroit's catcher, Charlie Bennett, who made ready to tag the King. By that time Williamson, who later confessed he had cut third by some fifteen feet, was near at hand as well. Bennett had the ball and was waiting for Kelly, but the King stood still and Williamson dove through his legs for the winning score.

Pete Browning is reputed to be the man for whom the very first Louisville Slugger was made. If so, he put it to good use, leading his league in batting three times during the course of his thirteen-year career. But if his alleged association with the famed bat is tinged with a bit of the white hue, another attribution might be even more apocryphal.

According to the tale, Browning and a teammate were sitting in a hotel lobby when they heard the news that President James Garfield had been shot. "That's awful!" said

Pete's teammate. "What's awful?" Browning wanted to know. "Garfield's been shot," the teammate repeated. "Gee," said Browning, "that's too bad. I guess I didn't know him. What league was he in?"

Chris Von Der Ahe, owner of the St. Louis Browns in the 1880s, was master of all he surveyed. He was the first great mogul in baseball history. One day he walked into his clubhouse and found that some of "his" equipment had been badly damaged. Summoning the members of the team, he demanded to know who had perpetrated such a dastardly act. No one answered. Then Von Der Ahe announced, "I'll give one hundred dollars to find out who did it." Another long silence, followed by a lot of fuffumping. Finally little Arlie Latham, the third baseman, stepped forward. "I know who done it," Latham volunteered. "Who was it?" said Von Der Ahe in his thick German accent. "Give me the hundred dollars first," Latham insisted. Von Der Ahe peeled off one hundred dollars from his wad and looked accusingly at Latham. Latham counted the money, tucked it into his back pocket, and said, "I did it!" Von Der Ahe let out a roar that would have done justice to an injured beast. "For that," he yelled, "I'm fining you fifty dollars!" And he stomped out of the clubhouse, satisfied that no one could put anything over on Old Chris.

For the last two decades of the nineteenth century, Arlie Latham was the most colorful character on the baseball landscape. A five-foot-eight pepperpot who made his name with the old St. Louis Browns of the American Association, Latham never, at least according to the stories he used to tell about himself, sat down. His energies were such that he looked like a man who had just taken a four-way cold tablet and figured he had three more ways to go to catch up with it. An agile tumbler—some suggested his skills had been honed by his having to leap from high windows when his adolescent courting was interrupted by the ultimely return of irate fathers—Latham could often be seen doing cartwheels in the field.

Once, in a game with the Chicago White Stockings, Latham dragged a bunt down the first-base line, in the direction of first baseman "Cap" Anson. As Anson approached the ball little Arlie flew headfirst over the stooping figure, landed on his hands and shoulders, and flipped himself quickly erect onto first base. With both feet safely anchored to the base, he saluted the Chicago captain with a "How do, Anse." The crowd howled its approval, but Anson merely tossed the ball back to the pitcher and returned to his position without the courtesy of a nod.

In 1882, Charlie Comiskey came up to the joke nine of the old-old American Association, the St. Louis Browns, a mere broth of a boy straight from the Dubuque Rabbits. By the end of his second year the twenty-three-year-old Comiskey had been made manager of the club—as well as its first baseman. Almost immediately he began to seek out talent, and it was an age when real material was as scarce as hen's teeth; every Tom, Dick, and Harry was employed to scour the bushes for anything resembling a ballplayer.

One bright day in June a steady patron of the Browns called on Comiskey. "I have a cousin," he said, "Andrew Jackson Jones by name. He lives on a farm near Joplin, but often comes to town to play at short for the Joplin Blues. I want you to give him a trial, Charlie. I'll bet the hair off my head he makes good." Comiskey, anxious for anything, gave his stock line: "If you think this Joplin terror is the goods, I'll give him a whirl at it."

Four weeks later the prospect and his grip came through the gate at old Sportsman's Park looking for the young manager—or "Commander," as he was called. Comiskey fixed him up with a uniform and sent him out on the field to face the Pittsburgh Brewery team—so called because they never went on the field without the contents of at least part of a brewery beneath their belts. They were sometimes awful, but on this occasion each man acted as if he had just sobered up and celebrated his newfound sobriety by driving the ball with fearful and awesome consequences. Several were directed at the aforementioned Mr. Jones, who managed to get in the way of the spheroid only to find it caroming off his knees and straight into his esophagus and other appurtenances.

After the game Jones came over to Comiskey, shook him by the hand, and said, "I done the best I know how. I don't know just what you think of me and my playin', but I ain't no fool. I know when I've had enough. All the same, Captain, I'm obliged to you just for the opportunity you gave me to make a damned fool of myself." And with that Jones turned on his heel and left the ball field. Forever.

Charles William Eliot, president of Harvard University in the late nineteenth century, was not what one would call a sports fan. At one point Eliot announced at the end of a successful baseball season that he was thinking of dropping the sport. When one of the supporters for what was even then billed as "the national pastime" pressed the president for an explanation, he replied, "Well, this year I'm told the team did well because one pitcher had a fine curve ball. I understand that a curve is thrown with a deliberate attempt to deceive. And surely that is not an ability we should want to foster at Harvard."

Many ballplayers are hard-pressed to have even one nickname. Frederic Schmit was blessed with two: "Germany," which he got by virtue of his ancestry and name; and "Crazy," which he came by honestly. Pitching for five years at the turn of the century, Schmit parlayed a lack of control and a high ERA into a lifetime record of 7–36.

Coupled with those two negative attributes was yet another, a poor memory. Whenever he pitched, Schmit would continually refer to a little notebook he kept tucked in his back pocket with his own notes on a batter's weaknesses. One day in 1893 the fabled "Cap" Anson—he of the three batting titles and 3,000 hits—stepped to the plate to face Schmit. Crazy turned away from the batter and took out his notebook. Studying it carefully for a few seconds, he read aloud his notation, "Base on balls." And with that he promptly walked Anson.

RAIN DELAYS

Back when men were men and women were darned glad of it, Amos Rusie stood alone as pitching's king of the hill. With seven straight twenty-game seasons under his perpetually gyrating belt—including three thirty-game seasons—and an average of 246 strikeouts over that period, Rusie was generally acknowledged to be the National League's premier barn-burner. The 1898 season looked little different, with the man they called "the Hoosier Thunderbolt" well on his way to another twenty-game season. Then Rusie's New York Giants journeyed down to Baltimore to play their hated rivals, the Orioles. With the game deadlocked into the ninth inning, Oriole manager Ned Hanlon sent in a new arrival, one Art Ball, to face Rusie's offerings.

Now Ball, just up from the minors, had heard many tales of the necessity of obeying orders in the majors if a player was to succeed, and he was determined to follow Hanlon's instructions to the letter. "What should I do?" asked Ball as he prepared to bat in the pinch. "Use your head," said the grizzled Hanlon.

The first ball that Rusie threw was wide. But the second came up with the velocity of a bullet, shoulder high, destined to become one with the strike zone. Ball stepped forward as if he were about to fire at the ball, but then stuck his head in the way of the oncoming spheroid. The ball glanced off, and Ball wilted into a heap at the plate. He was quickly taken to a nearby hospital for observation. After being unconscious for hours, he finally awoke to see his manager Hanlon staring down at him. Hanlon's first words to his now-conscious player were: "You dumb ass, you're fired!" Released from both the hospital and the team that very day, Ball never stepped in the way of another pitch.

Clark Griffith was called "the Old Fox" by sportswriter Hugh Fullerton, who claimed, "No brainier pitcher ever lived." Fullerton cited one moment in Griffith's twenty-one-year career that established his credentials as a "past master at handling batters in psychological moments." That moment came in a game in the early 1890s between Griffith's old Chicago White Stockings and the Washington Nationals. With two out in the bottom of the ninth and men on second and third, Washington needed one run to tie. Outfielder Kip Selbach came to bat. Griffith, who had won his spurs as a taunter of batters, delaying and stalling them to make them overanxious, immediately went to work on Selbach. "You big stiff," Griffith shouted at Selbach, "You couldn't hit this one with a hard board." And then proceeded to pitch one in high and wide. Griffith alternated the taunting and high, wide pitches with strikes until the count reached three and two. Now, with Selbach on his toes, wild with anxiety to get at one of Griffith's offerings, the Old Fox shouted, "Hit this, you big bloat," and forthwith delivered up a ball underhanded. The ball approached the plate so slowly that Selbach, in his eagerness to hit, fell to his hands and knees before the ball even reached the plate. He was called out on strikes.

In the early 1890s, teams lived—and often won—by their wits. Take the case of "Gentle" Jimmy Ryan and "Big" Bill Lange of the Chicago White Stockings team, who perpetrated a hoax to win a game. With the shades beginning to engulf the field and storm clouds gathering, Chicago had a one-run lead on Philadelphia in the top of the ninth, with two

Philadelphia men on and two out. As the last fringes of daylight were pushed aside by the coming darkness, the White Stockings pleaded with the umpire to stop the game, claiming they were unable to see the ball. But to no avail.

At that point, the Philadelphia batter smote a hard line drive to deep left field. Ryan, the left fielder, turned and ran back for the ball.

Sensing he could never catch up with it, he decided at that instant to put up his hands as if he were making the catch. Ryan turned around to face the field, pounded his glove the obligatory number of times, and then seemed to make the catch. Whirling, he pretended to throw the ball across the outfield to center fielder Lange, as he normally did when he caught a fly ball. Lange, having caught on to Ryan's ruse, carried out the charade perfectly, pretending to catch the ball and stick it into his back pocket. Then, followed by the entire team, he turned and raced for the clubhouse exactly as he would have had Ryan actually caught the ball. The pantomime was so good that no one in the grandstand or on the players' benches realized that the ball had actually passed ten feet over Ryan's head. The umpire, who only seconds before had turned down the request to call off the game, claiming there was enough light to see, had lost sight of the ball and was convinced Ryan had caught it for the final out. And every scorer in the press box was taken in by the deception, crediting Ryan with the out and giving the game to Chicago, 7–6, instead of Philadelphia, 8–7.

Great outfielders like Tris Speaker and Joe DiMaggio have bedazzled thousands with their ability to judge the force and direction of a batted ball from the sound and make lightning adjustments to it. Outfielders who cannot see the ball until it rises out of the shadows can still move in the right direction—or left, as the case may be—before they even see the ball in flight. In 1896, one outfielder, "Tacks" Parrott by name, playing for the St. Louis club in the National League, outdid all the rest. It seems that Tacks was playing center field in St. Louis, where the high grandstands cast a very heavy shadow. The batter fouled the ball over the stands and Tacks, hearing the crack, gazed rapidly in all directions in search of the ball. Then, espying what he took to be the ball, he turned and raced out toward center field. Leaping, he stuck up one hand—and caught a low-flying English sparrow.

"Special days" date goes as far back as 1883, when ladies were admitted free to the Polo Grounds to watch the Giants. Then, in 1889, the owner of the Cincinnati Reds discovered that when handsome Tony Mullane, known as "The Apollo of the Box," was scheduled to take his turn the stands were filled with hundreds of females. Soon the local papers were carrying small ads that read: "Mullane Will Pitch for Cincinnati Today!" Small print added the kicker, "Women Accompanied by Male Escorts Will Be Admitted Free."

The Washington Senators, then of the National League, saw the idea and raised it one. With Win Mercer, a handsome member of the pitching staff and the idol of the distaff set, well on his way to a twenty-game season, the management named one day each week, the day Mercer pitched, as Ladies' Day, females to be admitted free of charge. During one of his last appearances of the season, Mercer took exception to an umpire's call and walked in from the mound to offer the miscreant a pair of glasses. The ladies in the stands shrieked with delight. But the umpire was hardly amused. He forthrightly ejected Mercer from the game.

Once their reason for attending had been removed, the ladies unleashed all the fury they normally saved for Christmas shopping on the unfortunate umpire. Hundreds of infuriated females surged out of the stands intent upon nothing less than inflicting physical mutilation on the unworthy. Seeing the sea of parasol-wielding females descending upon him, the umpire made a mad dash for the office adjacent to the ballpark. There the front office staff shuttered the windows to save him from the stones and bricks that filled the air. Several of the ladies guarded the exit with clubs and bricks lest the umpire try to make his way out, while the office employees secretly ferreted him out of a rear door to a carriage drawn by a team of fast horses. The female mob hung around for hours afterward, weaponry at the ready, hoping to catch a glimpse of their hero's defiler. Thus was Ladies' Day almost over before it started.

Joe Kelley, the popular outfielder for the Baltimore Orioles, had been presented with a watch by his many fans before the start of a game. At the clubhouse door he gave the watch to an attendant for safekeeping until after the game. The clubhouse man, however, had to leave early and asked umpire George Burnham, who had just entered, to keep Kelley's valuable timepiece.

Along about the fourth inning, Burnham called Kelley out at second on a close play. The decision broke up the

Orioles' rally, and all the members of the scrappiest team in baseball history rushed at Burnham to argue the decision. Kelley was the most furious of all, adding his insights and outtakes, along with a few choice words, to the violent argument taking place around the ump.

Finally, the field was cleared of all but Kelley, who continued to follow the ump around the diamond, berating him. The hapless Burnham reached into his pocket and pulled out the watch given to him for safekeeping. "You've got just one minute to get back there and play," he said, "or I'll forfeit the game." "Oh, yeah," roared Kelley. And with that he slapped the watch out of Burnham's hand and kicked it across the field. "Now you *will* get out," Burnham snapped. "That'll cost you twenty-five dollars. And the watch'll cost you a hundred." "A hundred!" screamed Kelley. "Why, that Waterbury ain't worth three dollars," he added derisively. "Maybe not," Burnham retorted. "You ought to know, because it's yours. It's the one the Baltimore fans gave you before the game."

Forever after the umpire was known as "Watch" Burnham.

Rube Waddell told the story of how he came by the name "Rube" while pitching for the Oil City, Pennsylvania, team. "The man intending to pitch for us got drunk," Rube would tell anyone within earshot, "so I went in. In the second inning, with the score two to nothing against us, a lined ball hit me on the forehead and knocked me unconscious for about five minutes. I was sore and insisted on pitching out the game. We beat them sixteen to two and they did not get another man to first base while I made two home runs, two double baggers, and a single.

"That night the manager of the Oil City team met me on the street and said, 'You're a regular rube; no one but a rube could recover from an incident like that and finish the game.' And that fastened the nickname to me and it stuck."

When Richard William Marquard first joined the New York Giants, he quickly earned the nickname "Rube." One story illustrates how he came by the name. Just after coming up from the American Association, Marquard was seated in the lobby of a hotel, intently studying the box scores of a newspaper for familiar names. His eyes fell on a line at the bottom of the tabulation, which read: "The umpires: Messrs. Klem and Emslie." Marquard turned to a teammate, likewise absorbed in digesting the latest baseball tidbits, and said, "Is that guy Messrs. up here now? He umpired in the Association when I was there."

Johnny Evers was the party of the second part in baseball's most famous trio, the Tinker-to-Evers-to-Chance infield combination. The three players not only helped win four National League championships in five years, they became so intertwined in people's minds that they were voted into the Baseball Hall of Fame as a unit. Evers stood out from the others, however, not only for his size—a scrawny five foot nine, 125 pounds, with the physical construction of a baseball bat with a thyroid condition—but for his smarts. It was Evers who denied victory to the New York Giants in 1908 when he spotted Fred Merkle's failure to touch second base, necessitating a play-off in which the Cubs won the pennant.

He bedeviled the Giants on other occasions as well. Take, for instance, the Giants' use of the pitcher Luther Taylor, nicknamed "Dummy" because he was deaf and dumb. From 1903 through 1908, Taylor used a complicated set of signals developed for him by manager John McGraw to win a total of eighty-five games. But, courtesy of Johnny Evers, few of those wins came at the expense of the Cubs. Whenever Taylor pitched against the Cubs in the early part of his career, Evers, a noted hand-pirate, watched the strange goings-on intently. He was unable, however, to decipher the signals, as he had so many others. But when Evers figured out the nature of the signals, he took up the study of sign language, becoming so proficient that he could not only converse fluently with his fingers but also "listen" to the signs being flashed to Taylor. When the Giants finally discovered that Evers had broken their code, they had to resort to another set of signals, restricting their use of sign language with Taylor to social occasions.

Players have forever been the recipients of adoration and gifts from a grateful public. And so it was that after the 1906 World Series the entire populace of Wichita, Kansas, showed up for a celebration in honor of its favorite son, Chicago White Sox first baseman Frank Isbell, the batting star of the victorious "Hitless Wonders." Isbell, who sported the handle "the Bald Eagle," and for good reason, was given gifts worthy of a man voted most likely to recede—

including a real, live bald eagle, a bald-faced mustang, and a billiard cue ball.

Sam Leever pitched for the Pittsburgh Pirates for thirteen long, successful years. And after every one of those years, Pirate owner Barney Dreyfuss had trouble signing Sam up for the coming season. The Pittsburgh front office would dutifully mail a contract to Sam at his house back in Goshen, Ohio, but they would receive no reply. Finally, Dreyfuss figured out what was at the bottom of the annual holdouts. Thereafter, every year, Dreyfuss would address an envelope to Leever enclosing a two-cent stamp. When the stamp arrived at Sam's home, he'd mail back his signed contract. But not until then.

The 1908 pennant race is best remembered for one game, the one in which New York Giant rookie Fred Merkle failed to touch second base, necessitating a play-off between the Giants and the Cubs. There was another game between the two rivals during the same season, however, in which the unusual circumstances, if not the drama, equaled that of the later game. Earlier that summer the Giants were hosting the Cubs and, as the game went into the ninth, the Giants were four runs to the good. With right-hander Doc Crandall pitching well, there seemed to be little cause for concern. So little, in fact, that Christy Mathewson, the Giants' ace pitcher, who had been sitting on the bench throughout the previous eight innings, left to indulge in the luxury of a shower.

Within seconds after Matty had departed the bench, the Cubs, who would never say die—especially to a Giants team—began to rally, driving many of Crandall's pitches far afield. Before manager John McGraw could make a move, the Cubs had two runs in and as many men on base. McGraw sent out an S O S for Mathewson. But the big pitcher was nowhere to be found.

McGraw finally got the word to the pitcher, but then he faced a different problem: he had to delay for time while Matty got dressed. His ploys included arguing, visiting the mound, and every other trick he could think of as he played for as much time as possible.

Meanwhile, back in the clubhouse, Matty already had his shirt on. With two reserves acting as his valets, he was dressing as quickly as possible. The home plate umpire finally lost his patience, however, and ordered McGraw to play or forfeit the game. At this juncture McGraw sent out his other ace pitcher, "Iron Man" Joe McGinnity, to hold the fort. McGinnity took as much time warming up as humanly possible, but he was finally forced to stand and deliver. He pitched one ball, which Cub Jimmy Slagle promptly whacked over first to bring Chicago to within one run of the Giants.

Mathewson, meanwhile, couldn't find his trousers, even with a growing army of men to help him. He finally came running out of the clubhouse, half-dressed and with shoe laces untied trying mightily to fix his uniform. Running across the field with his uniform flapping in the breeze, Matty called out to McGinnity, "Hold up!"

Eleven minutes having elapsed since Crandall had been removed from the game, Mathewson was not given the benefit of a warm-up by the more-than-somewhat-miffed umpire, but was told to commence pitching immediately to the next batter, one Del Howard. Matty's arm was stone cold dead in the market. And so, unable to throw anything smacking of speed, he dropped three slow, twisting "fade-away" balls near the plate, two of them fading until they hit the ground. But Howard, too eager to wait Matty out, also lost his shirt—taking three desperate swings and striking out to end the game.

Baseball makes strange bedfellows. Or at least it did in the case of Rube Waddell and Ossie Schreckengost, Philadelphia Athletics battery mates in the first decade of the twentieth century. Waddell, called "Rube" and other less endearing names for his eccentricities, and Schreckengost, called "Schreck" by claustrophobic sportswriters anxious to fit his name into their box scores, both came to the Athletics in 1902 and stayed through 1907. For most of those years the two not only shared a room, but, as was the custom in the good old days, a double bed. Before the 1903 season manager Connie Mack heard that Waddell was unwilling to sign a new contract with the Athletics. Mack promptly called his talented pitcher to his office and asked him if it were true. "Yeah," said Waddell. "I don't wanna sign no contract." "You mean you don't think I'm paying you enough," asked the incredulous Mister Mack. "No," said Rube. "It ain't the salary that's bothering me. I won't sign no contract 'less it says that damn Schreckengost quits eatin' them damn crackers in bed." Mack stared at Waddell, not sure what he had just heard. But, after some more questioning, the gist of his pitcher's complaint came tumbling out. Waddell got along well with his catcher, except for one thing: Schreck's habit of taking a box of animal crackers to bed with him every night and eating them before he went to sleep. Since Waddell had to sleep in the same bed, he complained that the crumbs drove him crazy and that he wasn't going to put up with it any more. He wanted it spelled out in his contract that Schreck wouldn't "eat no more animal crackers in bed." And so Mack inserted a clause into Waddell's contract which read that if Rube's roommate ever ate animal crackers in bed, Waddell would be given a change of quarters. The contract became known throughout the baseball world as the "animal cracker contract."

Chief Bender was the mainstay of the Philadelphia Athletics' pitching staff for almost a dozen years, winning 191 games and leading them to five pennants and three World Series. It was his bearing both on and off the mound that made Chief Bender special. For this full-blooded Chippewa and alumnus of Carlisle School was a man of vast dignity. One afternoon that dignity was sorely tested as part of the opposing crowd repeatedly burst into war whoops in an attempt to unnerve Bender. Finally, deciding that he had had as much riding as the rules required him to take, Bender walked majestically to the first-base line where his tormentors were seated and addressed them: "Listen you ignorant, ill-bred foreigners! If you don't like the way I'm doing things out there, why don't you just pack up and go back to your own countries?"

Nick Altrock, who would gain later fame as a pitcher on the 1906 "Hitless Wonders," the world champion Chicago White Sox, and still later as a comic, was honing his skills with an outlaw team in Los Angeles back in 1901. Altrock deliberately walked the first seven batters to face him in one game and then promptly picked each one of them off first, offering up the reason, "It was the only way I could get those SOB's out!"

Jack Powell pitched for sixteen years in the major leagues, spanning the cusp of the twentieth century and becoming, along with Bobo Newsom, one of only two men to win more than 200 games and still lose more than he won. One reason might be that for the last seven years of his career, Powell pitched for the St. Louis Browns, a team that only once saw the light of the first division. But even in the twilight of his career, Powell possessed perfect control. Take the time he was pitching in front of his hometown crowd. And losing, through no fault of his own. The fans in one section of the bleachers were jeering Powell mercilessly. Powell put up with it as long as he could and then, singling out the man who seemed to be leading the hecklers, let fly with his fast ball. The ball sailed true, striking the jeer leader squarely in the mouth and knocking out his front teeth. The party of the second part, a man named Gleason, sued Powell. After listening to Powell's side of the story, however, the jury decided that the pitcher was justified in his actions and dismissed the case.

The 1908 Cleveland Indians finished a mere one-half game behind the league-leading Detroit Tigers. That's right, one-half game; rained-out games were not made up in days of yore. George Stovall, the Tribes' first baseman, attributed the loss to a pair of baseball shoes. At that time there was a billboard in Cleveland's old-old stadium offering a pair of baseball shoes to every player who hit a triple. "The boys," said Stovall, "had to pay for their own footwear and it was a costly item, considering the salaries paid in those days. Well, in one inning alone the first two men doubled and both were caught trying to stretch out the hit for a triple. Yes, sir," he concluded, "we finished second on account of a pair of shoes."

Wild Bill Donovan threw many pitches during his eighteen-year pitching career, but none stranger than the one Charley "Boss" Schmidt asked him to throw during the pennant race of 1909. During one game between the Athletics and the Tigers, with two strikes on the batter, Schmidt gave Donovan the pitchout sign. Donovan looked around to check out the situation, and then, assured that he was correct in his assumption that there was nobody on base, waved off Schmidt's signal. Schmidt gave it again. Donovan now pointed to the empty bases, one at a time, to reinforce his point and waved off Schmidt a second time. Schmidt, however, flashed a third pitchout signal. Donovan called time. The famous battery met halfway between box and plate, Donovan starting the conference with a "What-the-hell's-going-on-here?" "This fellow's been cussin' the umpire, and the ump just warned him that the next one's goin' to be a strike, wherever it is," answered Schmidt. So Donovan returned to the mound and threw the requested pitch, a pitchout, which umpire Tim Hurst, as advertised, called "strike three."

"Orator Jim" O'Rourke was one of the first stars of the old, old National League. An outfielder-cum-catcher who began playing ball in Bridgeport, Connecticut, the year after the cessation of hostilities known as the Civil War ended, O'Rourke by 1872, was playing for the Middletown Mansfields in the National Association. There he caught the eye of Harry Wright, who signed him to a contract to play for the Boston Red Stockings as a first baseman and substitute catcher. O'Rourke played in all seventy games in the first official season of the National League, 1876, and then, after leading them to two championships, moved over to the Providence team, where he was instrumental in their winning the championship in 1879. Hardly through, O'Rourke now moved on to the New York National League team in 1885, a team its manager proclaimed were "Giants in action as well as stature." And despite his stocky five-foot-eight, 185-pound frame, O'Rourke was indeed a "Giant," a regular on the 1888 and 1889 championship teams. O'Rourke continued playing in the National League through the 1893 season, compiling 2,654 hits and a .311 average during his twenty-two-year career in organized ball. He then "retired" to Bridgeport, Connecticut, where he organized the Connecticut League, serving as secretary-treasurer for the league and first-string catcher for the Bridgeport club.

Still, the old urge coursed through his veins. And so, when the 1904 edition of the New York Giants came within one game of clinching their first championship in fifteen long years, O'Rourke took it upon himself to be at the pennant-clinching game. But not merely as a spectator: Orator Jim wanted to be a part of the action. Approaching Giant manager John McGraw, O'Rourke pleaded his case, begging for a chance to get into the lineup on that afternoon of afternoons, if even only for half an inning. But McGraw would have none of it, citing the fact that O'Rourke was too old—even though Orator Jim claimed he was *only* fifty-two—and that he "ought to know better than to ask." However, O'Rourke wasn't about to give up, and he approached starting pitcher "Iron Man" Joe McGinnity. McGinnity, in turn, went to McGraw and talked the man known as "the Little Napoleon" into letting O'Rourke catch. And catch he did, not merely for a half an inning, but for the full nine innings, getting a hit and scoring a run for the Giants in their pennant-clinching effort. And becoming, in the process, the oldest man in major league history ever to play a complete game.

Like most pitchers, Rube Waddell of the Philadelphia Athletics prided himself on his batting prowess almost as much as his pitching. One day, with the score 2–1 against his Athletics, Waddell came to the plate with two outs and the tying run on second. At that moment the catcher of the opposing team tried to pick the runner off second and threw the ball somewhere in that general direction. The pickoff throw eluded the second baseman and wound up somewhere in center field. As the outfielders tried to hail the ball down, the base runner took off for the plate. He would have made it with plenty of room to spare if Waddell, still standing at the plate, hadn't stepped into the throw to the plate and hammered it over the left-field fence. Called OUT! for interference, Waddell returned to the bench to retrieve his glove, where he met his irate manager, Connie Mack. "Why did you do it?" moaned Mack. Waddell explained sheepishly, "They had been feeding me curves all afternoon, and this was the first straight ball I'd looked at!"

Clouds have been called the bladders of heaven, and the rains they release are a godsend to many. But not to baseball players, and particularly not to "Germany" Schaefer, who once petitioned to have a game called in a most unusual manner. But then again, Schaefer was a most unusual man, one who lit up baseball's skies during the first decade of the twentieth century.

On the occasion in question, a Detroit-Cleveland game, Schaefer had watched the steady rain come down for about ten minutes. The Tiger second baseman had continually appealed to plate umpire Tom Connolly for a suspension of the proceedings, but none had been forthcoming. Now Schaefer tried a new tack. Donning high rubber boots, a raincoat, a bright yellow fisherman's hat, and an umbrella, Schaefer came out onto the field. Approaching Connolly, he said, "I have a very bad cold and it's now bordering on pneumonia. If I get rid of my rubber boots, raincoat, hat, and umbrella, I'll be in the hospital in less than two hours. And," he capped his plea, "I'll sue you and the league for damages." That did it! Connolly suspended the game.

Plato didn't know "Rube" Waddell when he wrote, "Of all the wild beasts, the boy is the most difficult to manage." But if he had wanted references all he would have had to do was ask Waddell's manager, Connie Mack, who would have told him that Waddell was, like a little boy, an unwholesome companion for grown people. In 1905, for instance, after the Philadelphia Athletics had clinched the pennant, Waddell got into a wrestling match over a straw skimmer with fellow pitcher Andy Coakley on the Providence train platform and cost his team its best pitcher in that year's World Series.

Another time, when Rube was scheduled to pitch against the St. Louis Browns, the opposing pitcher, knowing full well Waddell's propensity for rube-foolery, challenged Waddell to a distance throwing contest for five dollars.

Several hours before game time, the two pitchers marched out to center field to start their contest. The Brownie pitcher threw first and made what he considered to be a fairly decent heave in the direction of home. Waddell curled his lips in disdain and asked for the ball, telling his "mark" something like, "If that's the best you can do, give the ball to someone who can really throw." With that, the Rube uncorked the ball homeward bound. The Browns' pitcher voiced amazement. "That was a lucky throw," he said. "Betcha can't do that again." And with that Waddell bettered his previous throw. Still, the Browns pitcher protested, and to prove that his prodigious heaves were no accident, Waddell continued to throw the ball all over the park for the next two hours. Finally, assured that the eccentric Waddell had thrown himself out, the Browns pitcher paid up the five dollars and hurried to the clubhouse to tell his teammates of his ruse.

That afternoon, to the wonderment of all, Waddell threw a shutout, striking out double-digit Brownies in the process. As Waddell left the field, he chanced to pass the Browns pitcher who had tried to tire him out before the game. "Say, that was a swell practice you gave me this morning. Here's a buck back for you!"

Christy Mathewson was baseball's beau ideal for the first decade of the twentieth century. And one helluva pitcher to boot. From the year of his ascendancy, 1901, through 1907, Matty won 174 games, about twenty-five a year, and struck out 1,371 batters, or 196 per season. One of those he numbered among his regular victims was Cubs shortstop Joe Tinker, who in Matty's words "looked like a cripple at the plate when I was pitching." Tinker's so-called "groove" was a slow curve over the outside corner, a spot that Mathewson found with remarkable regularity.

One day, after succumbing to Mathewson's slow curve three times, Tinker sat in the clubhouse putting on his socks when suddenly he clapped his leg and shouted, "I've got it!" Johnny Evers, sitting next to him, started at the shout and could only ask, "Got what?" "Got the way to hit Matty, that's what," answered the now self-sure Tinker. All Evers could blurt out was, "If you've found a way to hit him, why I'm from away out in Missouri near the Ozark Mountains."

But Joe Tinker, true to his word, had seen something. And the next time he stepped up to the plate, instead of taking his usual position up close in the batter's box choking his bat, he stood far back in the box waving a long bat. The catcher, Roger Bresnahan, thought nothing of Tinker's new stance and signaled Matty for another dose of the same prescription: a low curve. Tinker, expecting the curve, stepped into it—almost across the plate—and drove the ball to right field for two bases, winning the game. As Tinker drew up at second, he shouted toward Matty, "I've got your number now, Matty." And indeed he had, bedeviling Mathewson from that point on with his long "pole" and even driving one of Mathewson's offerings over Cy Seymour's head in deep center field for a triple—and the first olive out of the jar—as the Cubs beat the Giants, 4–2, to win the 1908 pennant in a game occasioned by Merkle's so-called "boner." And for the next four years Tinker continued to hit Matty as if he owned him.

Back in the days when baseball was the national pastime and vaudeville ranked not too far behind, any ballplayer worth his spikes combined the two, performing on the vaudeville circuit during the off season to supplement his income and extend his fame. One of the first to smell the grease paint was Adrian "Cap" Anson, the playing manager of the champion Chicago Nationals. Anson caught the fever in 1887 when he brought his Chicago team to New York and went to see a play called *A Parlor Match*. Invited backstage before the start of the performance, Anson was given a bit part in the show that evening: the foreman of a crew of workmen digging for treasure. When Anson appeared onstage, however, one of the workmen greeted him with the set line, "Good morning," then added "Captain Anson." The audience roared at the greeting, and Anson, totally flustered, forgot his one line and tried to exit, stage right. But the other members of the cast quickly surrounded him and began pummeling him with bladders and bouncing sawdust bricks off his head, making for one large—and friendly—riot scene.

That experience didn't cure Anson of his stage fever, however. A few years later he starred in a play called *The Runaway Colt*. The climax of the play called for Anson to hit a home run, dash off into the wings on his way to first, and reappear from the opposite wings in a slide into home. The actor playing the part of the opposing catcher would receive the ball from somewhere above the stage and thrust it in the direction of the sliding Anson, whereupon the umpire would cry out dramatically, "Yer safe!" and the curtain would descend, the show at an end.

One afternoon Anson ran into Tim Hurst, the famous umpire, and asked him to play the umpire part for one performance. Hurst agreed, and took his place behind the plate for the climactic scene. As Anson came sliding into the plate and the catcher slapped the ball on the hero, Umpire Hurst, forgetting for a moment where he was, screamed out, just as the curtain started to come down, "Yer Out!" But the cause was not totally lost; the Chicago Nationals soon changed their nickname to the "Colts" in honor of their playing actor-manager.

Umpire "Silk" O'Loughlin had just had a bad day, and that evening, feeling somewhat embittered, he bewailed the sad lot of an umpire's life to fellow ump Tim Hurst. "An umpire's life is worse than a murderer's," bemoaned Silk. "He is an outcast, a thing despised, loathed, hated. He dares not talk to any one; has no friends; cannot speak to the players; must hide in obscure hotels; conceal his identity; endure abuse, insults, and sometimes even assaults."

"Yis," interrupted Hurst, "but kin ye beat thim hours?"

The
Teens

Russell Ford was one of the new breed of pitchers who came on the scene after 1910: pitchers who doctored the ball, causing it to dip in more directions than Little Egypt, the Hootchy-kootchy dancer at the turn of the century. Ford's newfangled "emery ball" broke enough to carry him to twenty-six wins in his rookie year—and took his team, the 1910 New York Highlanders, to second place behind the powerful Philadelphia Athletics. Over in the National League the Highlanders' crosstown rivals, the Giants, also finished second, losing the pennant to the Chicago Cubs of Tinker, Evers, and Chance fame. And that set up a postseason interleague series for bragging rights to the island of Manhattan.

Wanting desperately to win what was then a series that ranked in popularity with the newly-minted World Series, the city series between the New York Highlanders (soon to become Yankees) of the American League and the New York Giants of the National, Highlanders manager Hal Chase started Russell Ford, his ace rookie. Giant manager John McGraw countered with his, Christy Mathewson. And the battle was joined for seven marvelous innings of no-run ball. In the eighth the Giants loaded the bases against Ford on three scratch singles before Ford bore down and retired the next two men. That brought to the plate Giant shortstop Al Bridwell, the same citizen who had driven in the winning run against the Cubs back in 1908 only to have it invalidated by Fred Merkle's base running—or lack thereof. Ford now threw Bridwell two inside pitches, running the count to 0–2. All of a sudden the ample form of John McGraw could be seen running out of the Giant dugout. Holding up an autocratic finger to call time, McGraw reached Bridwell and whispered in his ear. Bridwell nodded knowingly and stepped back in the box, leaving Ford standing out there all by his lonesome wondering what the big hullabaloo was all about. Now more than somewhat disconcerted, Ford threw another bad pitch, plunking Bridwell full in the brisket and forcing home the run that broke the tie.

Afterward, Bridwell admitted that McGraw's ploy was exactly that—a ploy. For while he was standing just astern of the batter's box nodding his head, McGraw was whispering, "How many quail did you say you shot when you were hunting last fall, Al?" Of such pantomines are baseball wins made.

One of the most famous plays in World Series history occurred during the sixth—and final—game of the 1917

Series. In the fourth inning of the game between the Chicago White Sox and the New York Giants, second baseman Edie Collins led off the inning by getting on base on a throwing error by Giants third baseman Heinie Zimmerman. Collins moved over to third on another error. Giant pitcher Rube Benton, bearing down, got the next hitter, Hap Felsch, to tap back to the mound. Benton fielded the ball cleanly and ran toward the third-base line, turning Collins back to third. He then threw the ball to Zimmerman, who was covering the bag. As Benton made his throw to third, Giants catcher Bill Rariden advanced up the line, leaving home plate unprotected. Collins, seeing that Zimmerman had both the ball and the bag, turned back toward the plate, and, finding it uncovered, set sail for home. Zimmerman found no one to throw the ball to and took off, chasing Collins—a man who had speed enough to steal 743 career bases—right across the plate. It was the first run in a game the Sox went on to win 4–2.

Both the fans and the press belled Zimmerman, making him the goat of the Series. One reporter, Hugie Fullerton, paraphrased Kipling's "Gunga Din," ending it with, "I'm a faster man than you are, Heinie Zim!" But Zimmerman, noting that nobody was covering the plate, asked, "Who was I supposed to throw the ball to? Klem?" And umpire Bill Klem, upon hearing Zimmerman's comment, could only add, "I was afraid he would."

John McGraw was, in the words of Joe Durso, "a master of the rough and tumble and the natural enemy of almost anybody who cared to look his way without affection," including Lady Luck. One time that Lady Luck frowned on McGraw and his trained pit bulls known as the New York Giants was in the 1917 World Series when they faced the Chicago White Sox and came up on the short end of the Series, two games to four. His opposite number was Clarence "Pants" Rowland, the manager of the Chicago White Sox and, until 1915, a professional fan, barkeep, and restaurateur from Dubuque, Iowa. In one of those improbable scenarios that make up the baseball landscape, his friendship with White Sox owner Charlie Comiskey won him the managerial position with the Sox in 1915.

Despite his lack of experience in the wars and wiles of baseball, the White Sox rose under his guidance from sixth in 1914 to third in 1915—aided and abetted in no small way by the addition to the roster of such all-time greats as Eddie Collins and Joe Jackson. Then, in 1916, the Sox moved up the ladder to second and capped it all in 1917 by capturing the American League pennant. In that fall classic, with Eddie Collins spearheading the Sox—and outrunning the Giants' Heinie Zimmerman across home plate with the deciding run in the sixth and final game—the Sox beat the Giants, four games to two. After the sixth game, as McGraw crossed the field in defeat, he chanced to cross paths with Rowland, who was on his way to his own dressing room. Rowland stuck out his hand and proffered his condolences, saying, "Mr. Mc-Graw, I'm sorry you had to be the one to lose." McGraw merely stared at the extended mitt and snarled, "Get away from me, you damned busher!"

Before the 1919 World Series everybody, including the White Sox, had heard that something funny was going on.

Before the first game of the Series, Chicago manager Kid Gleason called a clubhouse meeting and said, "Now, some of you fellows on this club have arranged to throw the Series." With that, the innocent players all looked up and said something that sounded like, "What the hell's this?" And, according to one of those present, pitcher Dickie Kerr, they could immediately pick out the culprits because all the players who were involved kept their heads down. From that point on, the players known as "the Lily Whites" knew who the eight "Black Sox" were.

George Stallings, manager of the 1914 "Miracle Braves," was one of a kind. One of the few managers in the history of baseball who managed in civilian clothes, Stallings would always sit in the same spot during a rally, afraid to move lest he break the spell, oftimes finding that his legs had gone to sleep. But staying in one spot was not his biggest superstition—it was paper. Any little scrap of paper. For Stallings had somehow divined that paper in front of the Braves dugout was bad luck, and he would have his charges pick up any errant piece that came wafting by. That prompted opposing teams to create paper blizzards that would keep Stallings' minions forever busy. If one little scrap escaped detection, Stalling's would let loose a roar.

Stallings was as sarcastic as he was superstitious. One day, after a pitcher from nearby Harvard had gone into a game and failed to retire any of the five men he faced, Stallings walked up to the collegian, stuck his face into the student's, and yelled, "Rah-rah-rah-rah," before retiring to his place on the bench, there to await the next Braves rally. Or watch for trespassing pieces of paper.

To say that Joe Jackson wasn't a Harvard grad would be understating the case. Unable to read or write, Jackson often hid behind his shroud of ignorance, preferring to let his bat do his talking. Take the time when he first came back to play at Cleveland after having been traded to the Chicago White Sox. One noisy heckler singled out Jackson wherever he went, in the field or in the batter's box, and repeatedly hollered out, "Hey, Jackson, how do you spell ignoramus?" This went on throughout the game, with Jackson ignoring the heckler—or pretending to. As Jackson emerged from the dugout with his famed tread-like walk and carrying three bats, he was greeted with the obligatory, "Hey, Jackson, how do you spell ignoramus?" Jackson paid it no never-mind but, standing pigeon-toed in the box, knees bent and eyes fixed on the pitcher, he stepped into the ball with a graceful swing and lined the first pitch to the far reaches of center field for a bases-clearing triple. Perched on third, he sought out the object of his disaffection. Spotting the heckler, by now red-faced with apoplexy, Jackson cupped his hands and bellowed, "Hey, fatso, how do you spell triple?"

Fred Snodgrass, who would be permanently belled for his infamous "muff" in the 1912 World Series, was one of the breed of players who would do anything to get on base. Up to and including getting hit by a pitch. In the 1911 Series between the Giants and the Athletics, Snodgrass had already gotten himself on base twice by getting hit, once in the opening game on a pitch by the A's Chief Bender and once in game two by Eddie Plank.

Coming to bat to face Bender again in game four, Snodgrass and Bender struck up a bit of banter, each trying to get the edge. Bender greeted Snodgrass with a "Look out, Freddie, you don't get hit this time," and let fly with a fast ball directed at Snodgrass's head. Snodgrass got out of the way, and fast. But as he got up and dusted himself off, he hollered out at the Big Chief, "If you can't push 'em over better than that, I won't need to get hit. Let's see your fast one now." "Try this one on for size," retorted Bender as he unleashed his smoke ball, dissecting the plate and leaving Snodgrass swinging at air. Bender, showing his even teeth in a grin, chortled and hollered in, "You missed that one a mile, Freddie." Two more fast balls down the middle and Snodgrass struck out swinging. As he walked back to the bench, Bender's eyes followed him. And then the Indian great added insult to the already injured Snodgrass: "You ain't a batter, Freddie, you're a backstop. You can never get anywhere without being hit!"

Casey Stengel was widely heralded as one of baseball's premier showmen. But nothing proved his showmanship more than an incident during a game in 1918. Stengel, long a favorite of the Brooklyn faithful, had been dealt to the Pittsburgh Pirates during the off season, and was returning to Ebbets Field for the first time. Although technically he had gone over to the enemy, his every move was still greeted with cheers. And, on his first time at bat in the top of the second, Casey didn't disappoint his fans. Striding to the plate, he acknowledged the cheering by doffing his cap— whereupon a bird flew out of his hair, circled the diamond once, and then disappeared into the wild blue yonder. Seems that Casey, upon taking his position in right field in the bottom of the first, had seen an injured sparrow wobbling along at the base of the wall. Walking over to inspect the bird, Casey picked it up just as the first Brooklyn batter stepped in. Hurrying to get back to work, Casey placed the stunned bird under his cap and took his position. Stengel later swore he had completely forgotten about the sparrow. But those who knew better swore it was his way of giving his former team "the bird."

Walter Johnson was one of the most soft-bitten of men, a gentleman and a gentle man. He was always timid about brushing back a batter, so many of his adversaries, such as Ty Cobb, would dig in deep at the plate, all the better to get a toehold on one of Johnson's fastballs. His gentle demeanor carried over off the field as well. One hot afternoon, as Johnson and his roomie, Joe Judge, were leaving their hotel, a boor cornered Johnson and began bending his ear. Finally, after an hour of nonstop talk, the pest relinquished his hold on Johnson. Judge, who had been watching it all, said to Johnson, "Walter, why'd you give a jerk like that so much time?" Johnson paused and then asked, "What could I do? He was telling me he went to school with my sister." "Oh," said Judge, "that's different." And then added, "I didn't even know you had a sister, Walter." Johnson smiled. "I haven't," he said.

Bugs Raymond would be a shoo-in for baseball's all-time, all-drunk team. In his spare time he also pitched for the New York Giants, from 1909 through 1911. To curb his drinking, Giant manager John McGraw not only sent his salary check to Raymond's wife, but also had a Pinkerton detective tail him from watering hole to watering hole to keep him out of mischief. But, Raymond, a wily pitcher and a wilier drunk, soon discovered his tail and made his personal acquaintance, befriending and besotting his perpetual guardian in the process. Upset with McGraw after a particularly tiring night on the town with his shadow—it was a case of the tail dogging the wag—Raymond refused to pitch the next day.

"You have to pitch," said McGraw. "I've already paid you. I gave the check to your wife this morning."

"In that case," screamed the irate Raymond, "let Mrs. Raymond pitch."

Before Al Schacht became known as "the Clown Prince of Baseball," he had been a pitcher. Of sorts. Schacht had come up with the Washington Senators in 1919, less as a reward for his glowing minor league record than in response to a growing pile of letters to club owner Clark Griffith recommending him—all written anonymously by Schacht. Now, in his first major league game Schacht had managed to hold the mighty bats of the Detroit Tigers in check for three innings.

As the rookie came to the plate in the third, the plate umpire, Billy Evans, addressed him: "Young man, have you thrown all your stuff yet?" "Yes sir, everything," answered the some-what-taken-aback Schacht. "Including your fast ball?" asked Evans. "Yes sir, I've thrown it at least ten times." With that, Evans depressed the valve on his chest protector, allowing all the air to escape, saying, "Well, I guess I won't need this then."

Connie Mack never believed in doing things by halves. Like the little girl with the little curl right in the middle of her forehead, when his Athletics were good, they were very, very, good. On the other glove, when his teams were bad, the word "horrid" would hardly have done them justice.

So it was that when Mack's 1914 edition lost the World Series in four straight to the almost talentless Boston Braves, he smashed his team into pieces like an expensive Ming vase. His 1915 team went on to make baseball history, becoming the only pennant winner to plummet from pent-house to cellar in just one short year, going from a 99–53 record in 1914 to a 43–109 record the following year. The 1916 team was even worse, winning just 36 games out of 153. But "Mister Mack," as he was called by everyone who could get within earshot, took it in stride, saying philosophically, "Well, you can't win them all."

By 1912 part-time comedian and full-time player "Germany" Schaefer's illustrious major league career was almost behind him, and he was now all part-time, splitting his time between filling in as a utility player and coaching for the Washington Senators. On a day in June, against the Chicago White Sox, Schaeffer could be found in the coach's box down at first, with a bag of popcorn in his hand to show his contempt for the enemy. As the batter, outfielder Danny Moeller, stepped into the batter's box, Schaefer turned around and faced the stands. Assuming an awkward stance and dropping his popcorn, Schaefer cupped his hands to form a megaphone and announced to the spectators, "This is the way I always stand when I want a man to hit a single." And sure enough, on the very first pitch, Moeller smote a single.

About a week after the Chicago incident, Schaeffer was coaching in a game against Cleveland. In the sixth inning outfielder Howard Shanks was at bat with two strikes on him. Schaefer yelled out to the Cleveland center fielder, "Back up, you idiot! Shanks always triples over the center fielder's head when he gets two strikes on him!" The center fielder yelled back a recommendation that Schaefer go somewhere on other—and while so involved, Shanks tripled over his head. Schaefer turned around to the stands, assumed a new sort of stance—almost that of a contortionist—and yelled out to the fans, "This is the way I always stand when I want the score to be six to three in our favor!" And sure enough, that was the final score.

Joe Jackson was one of baseball's purest hitters. He attributed his success at the plate to his bats, eighteen of them in all. Treating them as if they were persons, he gave them each a pet name such as "Black Betsy," "Old Ginril," "Big

Jim," and "Caroliny." And each, according to Jackson, had certain virtues as well as certain shortcomings. Speaking of Big Jim, Jackson said, "He's comin' along good for a young feller, but I ain't got too much faith in him. Trouble is he ain't been up agin' big-league pitchin' very long." At the end of the 1913 season some of his teammates watched as Jackson packed his anthropomorphic bats into several carrying cases. In answer to their questions, Jackson said he was taking them back to South Carolina for the winter. "Anybody with any sense knows that bats are like ballplayers," he said. "They hate cold weather."

Chicago White Sox pitcher Urban "Red" Faber's credentials include, among other feats, 254 lifetime wins, four twenty-game seasons, and twice leading the American League in ERA and twice in complete games. Put them all together and they spell Hall of Famer. But two things Faber was not remembered for were his speed afoot and his stolen base figures—although he tied the major league mark by stealing three bases in one inning on July 14, 1915, a feat tainted by an asterisk, however, inasmuch that Faber was wandering the base paths in hopes of being tagged out, thus causing the game to be called due to rain while the other team wasn't having any of it. Therefore, when he set out in the fifth inning of the second game of the 1917 World Series whither his legs would carry him in the direction of third it surprised everyone. Including Buck Weaver, who had already staked homesteading rights to the base. As Faber slid into third, the rightful occupant, Weaver, could only look down at Faber and ask, "Where in hell are you going?" The more-than-slightly-embarrassed Faber, whose flight of fancy had ended the inning, picked himself up and dusted himself off, answering only, "Right out to pitch." And pitch he did, winning the first of his three World Series wins in the 1917 Series—three times as many as the number of bases he stole that game.

The first two decades of the twentieth century proved that baseball not only built character, but characters as well. One of those characters was "Lord" William Byron, an umpire in the National League whose forte was singing a rhyme that referred to the skill, or even the antecedents, of the batsman. He once infuriated a batter by chanting, "He's rotten/He's rotten/Who's rotten?/I've forgotten." And by the time the batter had deduced what Byron was driving at, he forgot to get mad at him.

Another time he announced a cocky rookie as "Now batting . . . for exercise." And then there was the time "Wild Bill" Donovan was pitching in a game with Byron calling the balls and strikes. After Byron missed what Donovan thought was an obvious strike, Wild Bill rushed the plate screaming, "Byron, what's the matter with you? You're blinder than a bat today." That was Byron's cue. He promptly burst into melody, singing, "Oh, Bedelia, I made up my mind to steal you. . . ." Donovan merely turned back to the mound, asking himself, "How're you going to argue with a guy like that?"

When left-hander Harry Harper first broke into organized ball, it was rumored that he needed a road map to find the strike zone, his walks approaching double digits every time he took the mound. Even so, his manager at Minneapolis, Joe Cantillon, believed his young pitcher showed promise. With a sense of mission somewhat akin to that of a Joan of Arc, Cantillon sent his young hurler forth time and again, praying that he would beget the desired reaction. One cold and windy afternoon, as Harper committed crime after crime, Cantillon kept glaring at his young pitcher, beseeching something from him that was beyond his control to deliver. But Harper, true to form, continued to walk almost every batter he faced.

Finally, hoping to be relieved, Harper began looking into the dugout in hopes that Cantillon would remove him. But Cantillon was having none of it. After watching Harper silently plead his case for two innings, he shouted out to the mound, "I'm not going to take you out. Stay out there and throw. Maybe the wind will blow a strike over the plate for you!"

Graybeards who haven't yet been hit by an errant trolley car oftimes start a story "I 'member back when 'Germany' Schaefer stole first base . . ." and hurry to continue their narrative before they can be interrupted. For you see, back when Schaefer played for the lowly Washington Senators and their entire offense was a bunt and a stolen base—they stole 215 bases in 1911—he tried to generate the offense all by his lonesome.

One afternoon back in 1911, Schaefer was perched on first and Clyde Milan on third with the score tied in the bottom of the ninth and Washington desperately in need of a run. With two out, Schaefer took off for second, drawing scant attention from the White Sox catcher. On the very next pitch, he reversed his path, dashing back to first and sliding into the bag in the hopes of drawing a throw from the catcher and allowing Milan to come galloping across the plate with the winning run. Only trouble was, it didn't work; the White Sox catcher was having none of Schaefer's shenanigans.

Although Schaefer was credited with having invented a new ploy—one that was soon outlawed by the powers-that-be, whose idea of fun was wearing brown shoes—the truth is that the gimmick had been invented some eleven years before by Harry Davis of the Philadelphia Athletics, who had stolen second, then returned and stolen first. But in Davis's case his return trip had drawn the attention of the catcher—and a throw as well—which allowed the A's runner on third to score. Davis's successful execution of the gambit notwithstanding, Schaefer is still acclaimed as baseball's forerunner of "Wrong Way" Corrigan.

John McGraw would do anything to win. Anything. As a player with the infamous Baltimore Orioles, he often resorted to polite forms of larceny, such as holding a player's belt to prevent his advancing on a hit ball. As manager of the New York Giants, McGraw would badger umpires, needle opponents, and, if it helped, try to locate the secret map of chance—all in hopes of winning. One time he hired Victory Faust as the team mascot. Faust, a certifiable fruitcake, had assured McGraw that his presence with the team would mean a pennant for the Giants. McGraw saw his opportunity to inspire his troops with this good-luck charm, and kept him on his 1911 edition—even letting him pitch two games. His Giants won the National League pennant over their hated rivals, the Cubs, by seven and one-half games.

Another time McGraw, watching his team stumble through a long and prolonged slump, decided that his team needed a stroke of good fortune, especially on the eve of a four-game series with the Chicago Cubs. Now those old-timers who haven't keeled over under the weight of their collected memories might remember that back in those days any player who spied a truckload of empty barrels was guaranteed to get a hit that day. Before the first game of the series a truckload passed the Giants on their way to the park. The game was no contest, with almost every player on the Giants hitting the combined offerings of the Cubs's finest. The next day witnessed another truckload of empty barrels and, presto, another Giant win. Same scenario for the following day. Finally, on the fourth day of the series, one of the Giants dressing for the game looked up and saw a little man standing near him in the clubhouse. "Looking for someone?" asked the player. "Mr. McGraw," answered the stranger. "He ain't here yet," said the player. "Can I help ya?" "Nah," said the little man, "I'm waiting for McGraw. He hired me to drive a truckload of empty barrels past the ballpark every day, and I ain't been paid yet!"

Mordecai "Three Finger" Brown was the Giants' nemesis. Not only did he win the fateful play-off game necessitated by Merkle's failure to touch second back in 1908, but throughout the years all the pitcher had to do was throw his glove on the field to beat John McGraw's crew. One day "Rube" Marquard came into the clubhouse early and saw McGraw studiously gripping a ball. Looking up and seeing his ace left-hander, the man known as "the Little Napoleon" said, "I've been trying to see if it's Brown's grip, due to his loss of two fingers, that gives him that sharp break on his curve. But I've decided that it isn't," he said soberly. Then McGraw added, fixing the Rube with a baleful eye, "And it's lucky for some of you pitchers that I haven't, because if I thought it was his loss of two fingers that made Brown the pitcher he is, I'd get a hatchet and start working on you guys."

On that day back in 1894 when "Cap" Anson deputized catcher "Pop" Schriver to position himself at the base of the Washington Monument to catch a ball thrown by Clark Griffith from the observation deck, a new "sport," height-catching, became part of the early baseball culture. Trying for new height records became part and parcel of early baseball.

So it was that during spring training at Daytona Beach in 1914, Brooklyn manager Wilbert Robinson, responding to a challenge, attempted to break the record of 504 feet by catching a ball dropped to him from a plane flying at over 525 feet. Robinson, a former catcher for the old Baltimore Orioles, stationed himself under the plane flown by aviatrix Ruth Law. Instead of dropping a baseball, however, Ms. Law dropped a grapefruit. Robinson, unable to negotiate the right path to the descending object, stopped it with his chest and the grapefruit splattered all over him. Feeling the juice oozing over his prostrate body, Robinson screamed, "Oh my God! It broke me open. I'm covered with blood."

When told of the switch, he at first assumed that it had been the handiwork of Brooklyn outfielder Casey Stengel. But Ms. Law later revealed that neither Stengel nor any of the other players had had a hand in the substitution. She said that when her Wright Model B plane, engaged by the merchants of Dayton Beach as a tourist attraction, had motored to the end of the runway, she found that she had forgotten to bring along a ball. So, she went on to explain, "a man who had brought a small grapefruit in his lunch suggested that I drop the grapefruit instead."

Ty Cobb was the Howard Cosell of his day, always anxious to make himself conspicuous. One day, in a small New York hotel, Cobb called for the waiter. "Waiter, there's a fly in my soup," roared Cobb at the top of his lungs. The waiter hied over to where Cobb sat, looked down at the offending insect, and said, "Very true, Mr. Cobb. But why worry when there's not a chance in the world of you catching it?"

The Twenties

Tough George Moriarty was the only man to serve baseball as a player, a manager, and an umpire. It was during that latter tour of duty that Moriarty was found behind the plate when a brash Cleveland rookie stepped in to take his turn at bat. Moriarty called the first pitch a strike without protest from the rookie. But with the second strike, the rookie turned to Moriarty and politely asked, "Excuse me, sir, but how do you spell your name?" Moriarty obliged, spelling his name out letter by letter. The rookie sighed, stepped back into the box, and said ever so gently, "Just as I thought, sir. Only one 'i.' "

Fred Haney was a feisty little third baseman who plied his trade for four clubs over seven years in the 1920s. And while Haney managed to scratch out 544 hits during his seven-year career, his home run totals couldn't stand the vaguest sort of investigation, there being only eight to show for his efforts.

It was during Babe Ruth's record-setting year in 1927 that Haney, then a member of the Boston Red Sox, managed to hit his first home run in three years, a pop fly that barely carried over Yankee Stadium's low right-field wall. As the Yankee fans stood on their hind legs and hollered for less, Haney trotted around the bases, full of himself. At the inning's end, as the Red Sox took the field and Babe Ruth trotted in from right field, Haney couldn't resist needling Ruth. "Hey, Babe, how'dya like that? Now I'm only twenty-three behind you," alluding to Ruth's current total of twenty-four home runs. The very next inning Ruth teed off on Red Sox pitcher Slim Harriss and hit a cloud-buster to bring his total to twenty-five. As he toured the base paths, Ruth paused as he passed Haney. "How do we stand now, Kid?" he said, and proceeded on his merry.

With rare exceptions, the Boston Braves had been a losing proposition ever since the advent of modern baseball. Going back to 1901, the Braves had finished in the first division five times, two fewer than they had finished in last place. And their overall record for the first twenty-eight years of modern baseball was a less-than-sterling 1,734 wins and 2,450 losses, a .414 won-lost percentage, far worse than the numbers of the other two National League perennial losers, the Philadelphia Phillies and the St. Louis Cardinals.

Their losing record on the field was more than matched by their losing record in the front office, where no fewer than ten presidents had reigned less than supreme, their average tenure somewhat shorter than a home stand. The tenth owner of the Braves was an austere judge named Emil Fuchs, whose knowledge of baseball could have been entered on the head of a pin with more than enough room left over to inscribe the Lord's Prayer. Out of money and out of sorts, Judge Fuchs decided to take over the managerial reigns in 1929, aided and abetted by Johnny Evers of Tinker-to-Evers-to-Chance fame, who would try to make chicken salad out of the chicken droppings that Fuchs created.

One time during the '29 season, Fuchs watched as his group of have-nots, never-wases, and a few players who were not even household names in their own households, filled the bases with none out. "What shall we try now, boys?" Fuchs asked Evers. "What about a squeeze play?" responded Evers, baseball's early-day version of Billy Martin. "A squeeze?" asked Fuchs incredulously. "No, let us score our runs in an honorable way." Needless to say the Braves finished the season in last place and Fuchs soon retired to the front office to squeeze out some more red ink on the Braves' side of the ledger.

Little Andy High was just that: little. Standing but five foot six in his stockings, High was one of baseball's all-time lows, perhaps the smallest infielder in baseball history until Freddie Patek some three decades later. The St. Louis Cardinal, like many of his teammates, had a local business, an electrical appliance shop in the St. Louis area. Which promoted Charlie

Grimm, the resident wit of the Chicago Cubs, to comment, "Andy is the only electrician I know who has to use a ladder to put in a floor plug."

One of the pitching mainstays of the great Philadelphia Athletics teams of the late 1920s and 1930s was George "Rube" Walberg, a strong lefthander who won 134 games in the employ of the A's over the course of ten years. Walberg first came to the A's in 1923, waived by the world's champion New York Giants to the talent-thin A's.

A tall, gangling, overgrown lad, Walberg was determined to make a place for himself on Philadelphia's staff. It was during one of the games of his maiden season that the young player, pitching in relief, began staggering under the midday sun on one of those brutal summer days that seem to be associated with Philadelphia. Waving from the bench with his ever-present scorecard, manager Connie Mack called for his second baseman, Jimmy Dykes, to check up on the youngster. Trotting in, Dykes asked the gasping pitcher how he was, adding, "The boss wants to know. He thinks you're tired." Wiping the sweat from his face, Walberg panted back, "I'm great . . . I'll strike this guy out!" With Walberg's reassurance, Dykes waved an okay to the bench and started back to his position. He had taken about three steps when he heard the crowd collectively cry out "Ooooooh . . . " and turned around to see Walberg lying face down on the mound, out cold.

The Roaring Twenties roared a little louder because of the presence at the head of its passing parade of one man: Babe

Ruth. Ruth matched his on-the-field prowess with his off-the-field prowlings in pursuit of life, liberty, and whoopee. Ping Bodie, whose parceled piece of fame was that he was assigned to the same room as Ruth, was once asked who he roomed with. "With Ruth's suitcase," he answered.

Annie Oakley became part of the American language when, as the outstanding sharpshooter in Buffalo Bill's Wild West shows back in the 1880s, she took it upon herself to shoot holes in all free tickets given out to differentiate them from the paid-for ones. Down through the years, such "freebies" to entertainment and sporting events, complete with their punched-out holes, have become known as "Annie Oakleys." But Babe Ruth, who had trouble with all names— even forgetting the name of his center fielder, Whitey Witt— was unfamiliar with the slang term. When teammate Mike McNally asked him for a pair of Annie Oakleys for the new Follies show Ruth was appearing in on Broadway, Ruth replied with a hale-fellow bonhomie, "Sure, kid, I'll get you two of the swellest blondes in the show."

In the wake of the "Black Sox" scandal, baseball turned to Kenesaw Mountain Landis as their commissioner—and their savior. Landis, who had ruled against the Standard Oil Trust and several other transgressors from his seat on the federal bench, now dealt out penalties and punishments to all he viewed as defilers of the national pastime. One of the sins he came down hardest on was betting—especially on the ponies.

Calling National League umpire Bill Klem on the carpet for enjoying the inalienable right of any bettor to be wrong about horses, Landis demanded to know whether the veteran ump had, in fact, partaken of the ponies. "You're damned right I bet on the horses," stormed Klem in answer. "And I pay off a hundred cents on the dollar, too." Case dropped.

Paul Glee Waner started life as a pitcher, but he threw his arm out and turned his attention—and talent—to hitting. Thereafter he began to burn up the Pacific Coast League, batting .369 in 1923, his first year in organized ball. During that year, New York Giants manager John McGraw dispatched a scout to San Francisco to watch Waner in action. The scout saw a little five-foot-eight player weighing barely 150 pounds, sopping wet. He reported, "That little punk don't know how to put on a uniform." Two years later, McGraw personally scouted Waner, by now hitting .401, and promptly fired the scout for not seeing the potential in the future Hall of Famer. In signing off, McGraw said, "I'm glad you didn't scout Christy Mathewson."

One of baseball's greatest trencherman was Jack Scott, a pitcher of whom it was once said, "He would eat things you wouldn't dare go swimming with." The story goes that one year Scott reported to spring training unsigned for the season. Having won sixteen games the previous year, Scott thought he deserved a pay increase. Manager John McGraw of the Giants thought not. And there the battle lines were drawn.

But not the supper line, for when the dinner bell rang after the first day's practice, Scott dashed to the head of the line. The moment he reached his accustomed position, McGraw bellowed out, "Scott, get out of here! You can't eat at the club's expense." "But I'm starved," yelped Scott, who had developed a healthy appetite working out with the club that first day. "That's just too damned bad," answered McGraw, "If you're not working for us, you can't eat on us. No contract, no eats!" As McGraw turned away, Scott, taking one look at what he called the "vittles," wailed, "Okay, where's the contract?" While McGraw stood guard over the food lest Scott try to help himself to something on the old cufferoo, the contract was fetched from the office. With a borrowed pen, Scott signed and then hurried to the nearest groaning board to grab some vittles before everything disappeared.

Radio first burst onto the scene early in 1921, a revolutionary magic carpet that would soon transport millions of listeners to unimagined places—including the ballpark. In 1921 the first World Series was broadcast, sort of—sportswriter Grantland Rice phoned local New York station WJZ from the press box to report the going-on at the Polo Grounds between the Giants and the Yankees for studio announcer Tommy Cowan to pass on to listeners. Rice did the real play-by-play in 1922 between the same two teams. By 1923 NBC had hired radio announcer Graham McNamee, he of the bell-like tones, to describe the Series, again contested between the two New York teams. All afternoon McNamee wove word pictures, never letting the facts on the field interfere with his narrative. After the Series opener, an exciting game won by the Giants on Casey Stengel's improbable inside-the-park home run in the ninth, writer Ring Lardner, who had been seated cheek-by-jowl with McNamee all afternoon, got up and announced to one and all, "They must have been playing a double-header here this afternoon . . . the game I saw and the game McNamee announced."

During the early-morning hours one day at the Pittsburgh Pirates' spring training at Paso Robles, California, first baseman Charlie Grimm was awakened by beautifully played piano music issuing—loudly—from an adjacent room. Grimm finally arose and rapped on the door from whence the music came, telling the occupant in colorful phrases to cease and desist. Presently a stranger appeared at the door to inform Grimm that Ignace Paderewski was practicing one of his piano classics in accordance with an old Polish custom of warming up early in the A.M. "Well," replied Grimm, "just go back and tell Ignace Paderewski that it's an old baseball custom that Charles John Grimm *must have his regular sleep.*"

Arthur Charles Vance went by the improbable name of "Dazzy," a nickname he acquired mocking a cowboy who once said "Dazzy" instead of "Daisy" in his presence. But there were those who believed his nickname was a tribute to his dazzling fast ball, much as Denton True Young was called "Cy," short for "Cyclone." It was this fast ball, called by Vance his "swift," that took him to pitching's Triple Crown in 1924—leading the National League in wins with 28, in lowest ERA with 2.16, and in most strikeouts with 262—and took his team, the Brooklyn Dodgers, to within a game and a half of the pennant-winning New York Giants.

For his efforts Vance was named the National League's most valuable player, the first time the award was ever given out by the league. With the award went a thousand-dollar prize, in gold. The presentation of the award and the prize money was to be made at Ebbets Field by the president of the Baseball Writers, Fred Lieb. Lieb lived across from the old Polo Grounds and, like most New Yorkers, used public transportation, for the going price of five cents. On the day he was scheduled to make the award he took the elevated down to midtown and transferred to the Brooklyn-bound subway, all the while balancing the gold coins in his lap. "I just sat there and let people think it was lunch," Lieb was to recall years later. "Today you'd have Wells Fargo assisting Brinks."

Anything could happen in Brooklyn. And usually did. Take the year 1926. That was the year when Babe Herman, who was always there to commit blunders, crimes, and absurdities too numerous to mention, doubled into a double play—or doubled to load the base, third, if you're keeping score. That was also the year when, during one of Brooklyn's all-too-infrequent rallies, second baseman Chick Fewster decided to pound a bat on the dugout steps. All the better, he figured, to rile the opposing pitcher while urging on his teammates. Just as Fewster was in the midst of enthusiastically banging his bat on the front of the dugout, he heard the unmistakable voice of Uncle Wilbert Robinson, the manager of that menagerie known as the Robins. "Stop it!" Robinson hollered. "Why?" asked the amazed Fewster. "Ain't we got a rally going?" Robbie turned and nodded in the direction of his star left-hander, Jesse Petty, who was sleeping soundly. "I just don't want you to wake up ol' Jess," whispered Robbie.

Babe Herman was a rare piece of work, like no one who had traveled down the baseball pike before—or has traveled it since. He was the perfect leader for the group of losing stuntmen who in the mid-twenties played for the Brooklyn Dodgers—then called the Robins, in honor of their manager, Wilbert Robinson.

One day Herman was seated in the dugout alongside Robinson when a batsman on the opposing team hit a ball plumb perfect down the left-field line. Robinson jumped up, trying to gauge whether the ball had gone fair or foul. Unable to see the flight of the ball, he turned to Herman and asked, "What happened out there, Babe?" The Babe, involved at that point with a newspaper, looked up sheepishly. "I don't know, Robbie," he said, "I was reading the paper."

Wilcy Moore was one of the most unusual of rookies. A farm boy from Hollis, Oklahoma, Moore decided at the tender young age of twenty-five that he wanted to try baseball. And so he pitched in almost total anonymity for such clubs as Paris of the Texas-Oklahoma League, Ardmore and Okmulgee of the Western Association, and Greenville of the Southern Association. But even though every year was a winning one, it was almost a case of suppose somebody wins a game in a forest and nobody hears.

Then, in 1926, Ed Barrow, business manager of the New York Yankees, was reading the box in a southern paper and noted that a chap named Moore had pitched a very nice game for Greenville. The next time he looked at the paper he saw that the same Moore had pitched another nice game. Finally, after Moore had won twenty games, Barrow began to make inquiries. The reports were discouraging. Other clubs had passed on the big six-foot, 200-pound pitcher, who was nearly thirty years old, hadn't had too much experience, and didn't have the variety of stuff possessed by many of those already in the majors. But when the total reached twenty-five, Barrow decided to believe in the numbers rather than the scouting reports. Moore ultimately won thirty for Greenville and reported to the Yankee team of 1927, an aggregation destined to become one of the greatest in baseball history. Called "Grandpa" by his teammates, Moore made the team in more ways than one, winning nineteen games, thirteen in relief, with another thirteen saves.

Moore used his salary money to buy a farm, but he coveted something more: mules. The wherewithal was at hand in the person of Babe Ruth. For Babe Ruth would bet on anything, including some things that Bet-a-Million Gates wouldn't. And Moore had looked so awful at bat during spring training that Babe had bet Wilcy $300 to his $100 that he wouldn't get three hits all year. Moore took the bet and, lo and behold, got not just three hits but a total of six—in seventy-five times at bat—including one homer, to put him just fifty-nine shy of Ruth's total. Wilcy took his newfound $300 and bought two mules for his farm. One he named "Babe" and the other "Ruth."

When Joe McCarthy took over the reins of the Chicago Cubs in 1925, he was greeted by a group of athletes who believed in pulling themselves out of trouble with a corkscrew. The next year their ranks were joined by Lewis Robert "Hack" Wilson, then twenty-six going on Vat 69 and a player described as "a high-ball hitter on the field and off." McCarthy, who had come to believe that gin was no tonic for the Cubs' woes, took Wilson aside one day and asked him to witness a little experiment.

Arrayed on a table before Wilson were two glasses, one filled with water, the other with the best rotgut Prohibition bootleggers could gather on short notice. McCarthy took a worm out of his pocket and dropped it into the first glass and watched as the little worm wriggled its way around the bottom of the glass. Fishing it out, he then deposited it in the second glass, which held a potion the players fondly called "Old Panther Piss." The worm sank to the bottom of the glass and promptly expired. McCarthy proudly dug the worm out of the glass, and holding the dead worm in his hand asked Wilson, "There, Hack, what does that prove?" Wilson looked at the worm, looked at the glass, and said to McCarthy, "I guess, Skip, that proves that if you drink you'll never get worms."

Before pitcher Bill Henderson came up to the majors for that proverbial cup of mocha, he had banged around in the double A leagues for years and even caught on with the old Baltimore Orioles. Seems that Henderson was pitching for the Third Corps team during World War I when Buck Herzog discovered him and recommended him to Oriole owner Jack Dunn as possessing plenty of speed and curves. For a while he acquitted his buildup, but then, mysteriously, he became weak and erratic. A puzzled Dunn finally questioned Henderson's roommate, another former Army pitcher, "Cueball" Ellis, about the reasons why. "Shuah ah know," drawled Cueball. "That boy Bill's jus' one gamblin' fool. You know every time you give out meal money he takes it and gets into a stud game and the first thing you know it's all gone. He ain't got nothin' else so then he don't eat." The horrified Dunn dressed down Ellis, "You're a helluva roommate. Why didn't you lend him some money so he could eat." "Hell, I did," said Cueball mournfully. "That's why I ain't had nothin' to eat for two days either."

Back in the mid-'20s, a decade known as "the Era of Wonderful Nonsense," no team was more wonderful than the boys from Brooklyn, and none gave more color to "the Daffiness Boys" than Floyd Caves "Babe" Herman. Herman quickly became a Brooklyn favorite, revered for his shortcomings, which were many. Teammate "Dazzy" Vance, after having watched Herman fumble a ball with all the deference of a leper and then throw to the wrong base, said, "The Babe is a hard guy to out-think—how can you out-think a guy who doesn't think?" His base running also left something to be desired—like direction. Again Vance filled in the blank, calling Herman "the Headless Horseman of Ebbets Field."

One day Herman, feeling hurt at what he considered the personal and unkind criticism of his playing, approached one of the columnists. "You make me look like a clown all the time . . . Look, I'm a ballplayer. I make a living playing ball, like you make yours writing. And I got a wife and kids to support. If you keep on making fun of me, it's going to hurt me." The writer, feeling a measure of pity for the big guy, said, "I never thought of it that way, Babe. From now on," he promised, "I'll stop poking fun at you."

Herman patted him on the back, pleased that their little talk had proven fruitful. Then he proceeded to fumble in his pocket and pulled out the butt of a slightly used cigar. The writer made as if to get his matches, but Herman waved him off, saying, "Never mind, it's lit," and then puffed a few times to prove his point. The writer, who only a few seconds before had felt contrite, roared, "It's all off. Nobody who carries lit cigars around in his pocket can tell me he isn't a clown!"

Not everybody was impressed with Babe Ruth's sixty homer back in 1927. Years later the pitcher who had given up the monumental hit, Tom Zachary of the Washington Senators, looked back and said in his best North Carolinian twang, "Heck, if I'd a known it was gonna be a famous record, I'd a stuck it in his ear."

Jimmy Dykes was known as an umpire-baiter *par excellence*. But once, just once, he was brought up short by an umpire. And appreciated it.

The momentous event took place back when Dykes was playing for the old Philadelphia A's, a team then in permanent possession of last place. The third baseman stepped into the batter's box and watched the first pitch go by. "Strike one!" shouted plate umpire Bill Guthrie. The second pitch came by in exactly the same spot, with the same result: "Strike two!" Dykes stepped out to confront Guthrie. But before Dykes could say a word, Guthrie spoke. "What was the matter with that?" he asked, inviting a reply. Dykes obliged. "I thought it was a little high." Guthrie came back, "Son, you just keep on swinging and nobody but me, you, and the catcher will ever know you're losing your eyesight!" Dykes, for perhaps the only time in his life, was dumfounded. When he recovered from his shock he indulged in a hearty roar of laughter and then finished his turn at bat by flying out.

When Dykes returned to the bench he explained his actions to his bewildered manager, Connie Mack. "I know it was a serious situation, Mr. Mack, but I simply couldn't help laughing," he said. The sober Mister Mack, who had listened attentively to Dykes's explanation for his behavior, leaned back and said, "By golly, that was a good one, wasn't it?" And he smiled for the first time in years.

When Leo Durocher was first brought up by the Yankees back in 1928 to replace Mark Koenig, Miller Huggins decided to make him a switch hitter. "Why?" one of the writers' colony wanted to know. "Two reasons," replied Huggins. "I learned to do it when I was a kid. I was a weak hitter, smaller than Leo." "And the other reason?" the scribe asked. "Look at his average," Hug sighed. "What can he lose?"

And so Durocher began to take lessons swinging from the first-base side of the plate, working hard at it. But what, indeed, did he have to lose? He had batted .253 at St. Paul the previous year and he was now being called on to spell Koenig, who had batted .285 with the '27 Yankees—and not incidental to our story, batted from both sides of the plate.

But there didn't seem to be any way for Durocher to become proficient from both sides. He connected well enough swinging left-handed, but the ball didn't seem to jump off his bat with the elasticity of his right-handed drives— infrequent as they were. Finally, just as the Yankees were breaking spring training camp, the brash youngster boasted to the assembled writers, "I'll be the Yankees' first four-hundred hitter." "When?" was among the many four-letter words offered in reply. Durocher held his ground. "This year," he said. "Two hundred righty, two hundred lefty. That's four hundred, ain't it?"

T he Brooklyn Robins had made one helluva run at the New York Giants in 1924, finishing but one-and-a-half games back of their hated rivals in their drive for the pennant. Then, in an attempt to pass them, they began to scour the landscape for young talent, preferably pitching talent to help their threadbare pitching staff—consisting of just two arms, "Dazzy" Vance and Burleigh Grimes. One of those they brought to spring training in '25 was a young right-handed pitcher named Harry Ellenberger, summoned up from Johnstown. Wilbert Robinson, the Robins' manager—and the man, not incidentally, after whom the Robins were named—had just begun to share his managerial duties with his outfielder,

Zack "Buck" Wheat, figuring it would take two to keep tabs on the managerie in the Robins' zoo. But evidently Ellenberger never heard of the arrangement. After he had been in training camp for several weeks he approached one of the writers covering the team and asked, "Hey, pal, what does ol' Buck do around here?" In painstaking detail, the writer went through the ins and outs of the arrangement that had Wheat and Robinson both working the managerial side of the street. For a moment Ellenberger seemed satisfied with the explanation. But soon he was frowning again. "There's another thing I'd like to know," he said, invoking the help of the writer again. "Who the hell's that fat guy who's always popping off?" pointing to the roly-poly Robinson. Ellenberger was soon on a train back to Johnstown.

From the time Waite Hoyt had first appeared on the Major League scene as a nineteen-year-old schoolboy straight out of Brooklyn's Erasmus High, his fast ball had been his constant companion. But, as it must to all men after eleven years in the majors, his speed had begun to desert him and by 1929 the former "Schoolboy's" fast ball was little more than a rumor. Pretty soon the rumor had spread, and everyone began to hear about it, including New York Yankee rookie Sam Byrd. On a Pullman jump west from Philadelphia, where Hoyt that afternoon had been beaten by a ninth-inning home run off the broadest back of the A's broad-backed attack, Jimmie Foxx, Byrd came over to sit next to Hoyt. "Waite," said the rookie, "Whatever became of that fast ball of yours?" "Sonny," said Hoyt, fixing his eyes on Byrd, "you'll probably find it bouncing around upstairs at Shibe Park right now."

When Mel Ott first came to the New York Giants in 1925, he was a callow youth of but sixteen years. The boy was promptly dubbed "Master Melvin" and put on the bench next to Giant manager John McGraw for instruction. And safe-keeping. Day after day McGraw would impart his not incon-siderable knowledge and every day Master Melvin would take it all in, nodding and asking few questions. One day McGraw turned to Ott, who had come up as a catcher, and asked him if he had ever played the outfield. Ott thought about it and then replied, in all seriousness, "Yes sir, back when I was a kid."

Walter "Duster" Mails took a burning fast ball and an unquenchable ego as far as they could go, becoming one of the pitching mainstays for the Cleveland Indians in the early twenties before opposing batsmen began to make free with his pitches. Then the man who had dubbed himself "the Great" disappeared from the major league scene (although he reemerged three years later for one season), leaving behind him a reputation for eccentricity unmatched in base-ball annals. And the stories to prove it. One story had Mails, by now pitching somewhere south of the Big Leagues in the bushes, on the hill for one of the many minor league clubs he graced with his presence. The opposing club sent a formida-ble pinch hitter to bat against the eccentric southpaw. Grabbing the announcer's megaphone, Mails announced to one and all "The Great Mails will now fan the batter on three pitches." Mails made good on his boast.

According to wit Heywood Broun, being left-handed was merely a state of mind. However, down through the ages southpaws have acquired another reputation—for thinking left-handed as well. How else can one explain the antics of such southpaws as "Rube" Waddell, Lefty Gomez, Bill Lee, and others? Of course, Lee had an answer to being called a flake, asking "What can you expect from a northpaw world?" The time-honored struggle between left-handers and right-handers was best illustrated by an incident that occurred between two members of the St. Louis Cardinals pitching staff back in 1921. The Cardinals were en route to an away game and a card game had broken out on the Pullman. Jeff Pfeffer, the Cardinal right-hander, was one of the group playing and Bill Bailey, a left-hander, was kibitzing on the periphery, trying to get a seat in the game. Standing behind still another Cardinal lefty, Willie Sherdel, and watching him play out his hand, Bailey was moved to exclaim, "Gee, Willie, that sure was a rotten play. You play more like a right-hander than a southpaw." Pfeffer looked up. "Think southpaws are pretty clever, don't you, Bill," he said to Bailey. "Well," shot back Bailey, "you never saw one digging a ditch, did you?" Everybody laughed at Bailey's rejoinder, including Pfeffer, who, not looking up, offered, "Nope. But that's 'cause they want the ditches straight."

Even though the New York Yankees were the cock of the American League walk back in the '20s, manager Miller

Huggins was constantly on the lookout for new talent, talent he hoped would help his Yankees continue as kings of the mountain. So it was that one year he brought a pitcher named George Quinn, recently of the Wilson club in the Virginia League, to spring training. About halfway through spring training, Huggins called Tom Clarke, the manager of the Wilson club, to inquire about Quinn. "Say," intoned Huggins, "what's the story with this Quinn fellow?" "A nut, but otherwise he's a pretty fair right-handed pitcher," answered Clarke. "That's all I wanted to know," Hug replied. "He's been pitching left-handed ever since he's been here and you can have him back in the morning." When he rejoined the Wilson club, Quinn had an explanation for his behavior at the ready: "You don't think I was going to show that guy Ruth all my best stuff, do you?" he asked scornfully. "I was just keeping the right wing in reserve so's I could fool 'em better."

Rogers Hornsby was one of the greatest hitters in the history of the National League, if not the whole of baseball. A right-handed batter who stood deep in the batter's box, all the better to get a long look at the incoming ball, Hornsby would stride into the ball at the last nanosecond, his eyesight and stance ensuring solid contact with the ball. Unaccustomed as he was to striking out, one pitcher had Hornsby's number, Brooklyn Robins' fast-baller "Dazzy" Vance. One afternoon, after Hornsby had gone down swinging three times in a row against the offerings of Vance, one of Brooklyn's faithful got up and yelled, "Hey, Hornsby, ya bum ya, I paid good money to see ya hit!" Hornsby howled back,

"You've got no squawk coming. You paid to see that fellow Vance pitch, too, didn't you?"

His glory days long behind him, Casey Stengel had been laboring in the vineyards and backyards of baseball for most of his ten-year Major League career. Now he was on the woebegone Philadelphia Phillies, permanent possessors of the National League cellar. With little or no incentive, the peppery Stengel seemed to be playing out his career, going through the motions without the accompanying emotions. But, on the afternoon of July 1, 1921, there came a wire bearing news that most players only dream of: Stengel had been traded from the last-place Phillies to the first-place New York Giants. Suddenly, Stengel was a new man. As the Phillies, *tout ensemble,* watched his transformation, Stengel jumped up on top of a rubbing table in the dressing room and began indulging in some intricate calisthenics. His lips began moving as well. "Loosen up, muscles!" Stengel exhorted his battered body softly, "You're going to New York."

To his fans John McGraw was "the Little Napoleon." To his detractors, "Mugsy." And to everyone who saw him in action, baseball's version of Rumplestiltskin, constantly jumping up and down from the dugout with signals for every ball pitched. It got on everyone's nerves, his own players included, several of whom found it irritating and middlesome. One of those who took umbrage at continually having to look toward the Giant bench for instructions was third baseman

Freddie Lindstrom. Never one to hide his feelings, Lindy let several of his teammates—and even McGraw himself—know that the bench signals had gotten under his skin.

During spring training one year McGraw decided to position himself in the center field bleachers, the better to watch his troops in action from a different perspective. As luck would have it, Lindstrom, who had been shifted to the outfield, was playing center. On the day in question, Mrs. McGraw, who was seated adjacent to the Giants' dugout, decided to send her husband a note between innings. And who better, she reasoned, to use as a courier than center fielder Lindstrom? "Freddie, come here!" she beckoned. But Lindy didn't hear her call. So, the first lady of the Giants repeated her summons, only louder: "Freddie, can't you hear me?" That was enough for Lindstrom, who stared and then shot back, "Good grief, Mrs. McGraw, are you giving signs on this club, too?"

Back when the New York Yankees were known as "the Bronx Bombers" with good reason—the reason being Ruth, Gehrig, Meusel, Lazzeri, et al.—they played an exhibition game with the University of Texas. The Texas pitcher was holding the big bats of the Bombers pretty quiet for five-plus innings when, in the sixth, Lou Gehrig came to the plate with a couple of Yankees on base. The count went to three and two on Gehrig when, inexplicably, the Texas pitcher grooved one. The result was almost as predictable as one of Newton's laws. As the pitcher turned slowly and watched the ball disappearing from sight beyond the railroad tracks which ringed the stadium, the Longhorn catcher, in a rage, rushed out and demanded: "What the hell did you groove that ball for, you lunkhead! You might have known that guy would drive it a mile." The pitcher, sighing the sigh of contentedness, turned slowly and said to his disapproving catcher, "I know, I know. But I just got to thinkin'. I'll never pitch in the big leagues. I'll probably never even see Yankee Stadium. And I sure did want to see Gehrig bust one!"

Charles "Red" Ruffing would win 273 games during his twenty-two-year major league career, enough to earn him a place in the Hall of Fame. But Ruffing was not always a winner. His career began with the Boston Red Sox, then the most anemic team in baseball. During his rookie season in 1925, Ruffing was called upon to relieve between starts. And so it was that one day he found himself out in the bullpen, watching the game in progress and munching on a sandwich he had brought to the park with him. Before he could get halfway through it, the opposing New York Yankees had gotten to the starter and Ruffing was called upon to come in in relief. As he started his long walk to the mound, he turned around and said to his fellow bull-mates, "Who's coming up to bat for the Yankees?" Someone said, "Ruth, Gehrig, and Meusel." Ruffing walked back, wrapped up the rest of his sandwich, and admonished those still sitting in the bullpen, "Don't anybody touch that, I'll be right back."

Robert Roy Fothergill came by his nickname, "Fats," somewhat dishonestly. For while he stood more than five foot ten and weighed in at 230 pounds, Fothergill was less fat than a hulking mass with shoulders as big as hams—hams large enough to serve at a sit-down dinner for six—and the sort of substantial head you break a door down with. In short, he looked like a man who'd be more at home boosting kegs on and off a dray wagon than hefting a bat. His bat, by the way, was one of the largest ever known to the game, but in Fothergill's massive hands it looked like a little wand. He wielded it effectively, batting over .300 for eight straight seasons.

Breaking into the majors in 1922 as a pinch hitter for Detroit Tiger manager Ty Cobb, Fothergill became one-fifth of one of the greatest hitting outfields of all time, an outfield that included Harry Heilmann, Heinie Manush, Bobby Veach, and Cobb. Over the five-year period from 1922 through 1926, the quintet had a combined batting average of .352. But Fothergill not only used his bat to good advantage, he also used his manly bosom, skidding across the greensward for low line drives in a toboggan slide. On the base paths, he used whatever it took, once confiding to a reporter, "Feet were made to get you where you're going, but when they fail other means must be employed."

It was during the mid-twenties that Heilmann and Fothergill began rooming together. They took long walks in the evening as part of their daily exercise. One evening in Chicago, while the summer sunlight still clung to everything, as if accidentally entangled in the trees, they turned the corner of a street just off the Loop. In front of them stood a man bandaged from head to toe, propped up on two crutches. Heilmann, restraining his astonishment, said, "I wonder what happened to him." Without breaking stride, Fothergill responded, "He probably thought I was going to slide."

Jimmie Foxx, also known as "the Beast," and "Double X," broke into the majors as a plain, old ordinary Fox. But one day a Philly baseball author spied the name "FOXX" on Jimmie's suitcase. Asked the reason for the double X, Foxx replied, "Search me. But that's how my grandpappy spelled it, so I reckon it belongs there." And "Double X" it became.

Babe Ruth suffered some of the same humiliations as lesser mortals in flannels when he faced the offerings of Walter Johnson. One time against the Senators' fast-baller, Ruth took three straight fast balls for a called strikeout. As he left the plate, Ruth asked the umpire if he had seen any of them. "No," answered the umpire honestly. "Neither did I," replied Ruth, "but that last one sounded kinda high to me."

The Thirties

Ernie Lombardi was known as a base runner who could stretch a double into a single. One time a reporter at the Polo Grounds was too busy pounding the keys of his typewriter to keep up with the action and missed Ernie Lombardi's turn at bat. He looked up to see the lumbering Giant catcher perched on first. "How did he get on?" he inquired of the next inmate in the press box. "He beat out a hit to deep center," came the reply.

Charlie Grimm managed the Chicago Cubs for fourteen years, experiencing the full range of success, with teams that finished first and dead last. It was during one of the more barren periods of his stewardship that a scout phoned him excitedly to tell him about his discovery somewhere in the sticks. "Charlie," he hollered, "I've landed the greatest young pitcher in the land. He struck out every man who came to bat—twenty-seven in a row. Nobody even got a foul until two were out in the ninth. What shall I do?" Grimm, who belied his name, retaining his sense of humor in a time that would try men's souls, shot back, "Sign up the guy who got the foul. We're looking for hitters."

Detroit Tiger second baseman Charlie Gehringer was a quiet man, to put it mildly. In fact, quiet was the only noise he didn't mind. Gehringer was never heard to say an encouraging word; or a discouraging word, for that matter. Some even aver that he never said a word of any kind. As the fates would have it, Gehringer's roommate for seven years was pitcher Chief Hogsett, another nominee for clam of the year. In all the years the two roomed together they never came to words.

Except once. That exception occurred during the course of a normally taciturn meal, when Hogsett leaned across the table and said, "Charlie, please pass the salt." Gehringer stiffened and made no effort to comply with the request. The meal continued as it had started: in silence. Finally, a hurt Hogsett asked Gehringer, "Did I say anything wrong, Charlie?" Gehringer, after a moment's consideration, replied, "You could have pointed."

The Chicago Cubs of the mid-1930s were one of the most rollicking, boisterous crews ever assembled this side of the

H.M.S. *Bounty*. Their language would have caused a Billingsgate fisherman to blush, and their demeanor would have caused a prison riot to look well-behaved. Time and again they would try to bait the opposing team, hurling out a string of florid libels at everyone they faced. One of the objects of their disaffection was Waite Hoyt, by now at the end of his marvelous pitching career and putting in his servitude with the 1933 Pittsburgh Pirates.

As the decibel level of the Cubs's dugout rose and his ears began to burn, Hoyt, who had been a member of the fabled "Murderers' Row" teams of the Yankees but a few years before, remembered the Cubs's lack of success riding the Yankees in the World Series the previous year. Calling time, he strode over to the Cubs's dugout. And with hands on hips, confronting his tormentors, Hoyt shouted out, "Better cut it out, or I'll put on my old Yankee uniform and scare the shit out of you." With that, he walked back to the mound to the hush of silence.

Fresco Thompson was one of those journeyman infielders during the late 1920s and early '30s who won a reputation as a "good field–no hit" player. And an even bigger reputation for a quick tongue. Traded from the Philadelphia Phillies to the Brooklyn Robins in 1931, Thompson chanced to find his locker situated next to that of full-time slugger, part-time fielder Babe Herman. Herman greeted his new teammate with a "It's a helluva note to dress with a .250 hitter." Without batting an eye, Thompson shot back, "How do you think I feel dressing with a .250 fielder?"

By 1934 Thompson's career was winding down to a

RAIN DELAYS

precious few games. He spent most of his time relaxing on the bench, his duties those of a spot player at best. One afternoon, during an exhibition game, Thompson, now a member of the New York Giants, was called upon by manager Bill Terry to go in as a pinch hitter. Thompson leaned back, stretched, and called out to Terry, "I'd love to, Bill, but I just had my shoes shined."

Bob Feller was one of the most highly touted phenoms ever to come across the major league landscape. The very first time the great pitcher-to-be was outfitted with a uniform by Cleveland trainer Lefty Weisman, Feller complained about the fit of his cap. "Seems a little big," Feller groused. "See that it stays that way," snapped Weisman.

In the 1930s the Yankees wound down their spring training with a tour of Puerto Rico. The leading manufacturers on the island wined and dined the world champions, with everyone standing in line to host a dinner or sponsor an outing. One of the firms that entertained the Yankees was Don Q. Rum, which hosted a massive dinner thanking the Bronx Bombers for coming to their island. One by one the Yankees got up to thank their hosts for the banquet and express their appreciation for the warm welcome given them by the baseball fans of Puerto Rico. Finally, it came down to Lou Gehrig, who spoke last, as befitted the captain of the Yankee team. As Gehrig got up to speak, he mixed up his rums, thanking instead Baccardi Rum. Every time he got to a spot in his speech where he was supposed to mention his host, he said the name Baccardi, and one of his hosts, sitting nearby, would hiss "Don Q., Don Q.," to which Gehrig would answer graciously, "You're welcome." He'd then proceed to mention Baccardi again, prompting the host to hiss "Don Q.," and the roundelay "Your welcome" from Gehrig continued, on and on.

The New York Yankees were in Philadelphia for the first time in 1938 to play against the Athletics, and, as was the custom, the first lieutenant and coach of the A's, Earle Mack, Connie's son, had just gone to pay his respects to the manager of the reigning world champions, Joe McCarthy. "How's everything, Earl?" McCarthy asked. "Fine," returned the younger Mack enthusiastically. "I want you to watch our new second baseman, this kid Lodigiani. He's great, fast, goes to his right and left, clicks on double plays, and hits all kind of pitching." And in that first series between the two clubs the youngster did everything he was supposed to do, living up to his advance billing, even beating the Yankees with a home run in one game.

But after the Bronx Bombers had left town the rookie predictably let down, unable to keep up with the fast pace he had set for himself or the build-up Earl Mack had given him. Just two weeks later the A's returned the compliment, coming to Yankee Stadium for the second intraleague series. "How's everything going, Earl?" asked McCarthy, giving his normal greeting to visitors in the Yankee dugout. "Oh, all right," replied Mack, adding, "but we're a little weak around second base."

For five and one-half innings the Detroit Tigers faithful had sat sullenly through a long, frustrating afternoon watching their beloved Tigers get the bejabbers beaten out of them by Dizzy Dean and the St. Louis Cardinals in the seventh and deciding game of the 1934 World Series. Up 7–0 going into the Cardinal sixth, the Cards added yet another two runs on a Pepper Martin single and a triple by Joe Medwick. As Medwick came roaring into third base, Tiger third baseman Marv Owen apparently spiked him and Medwick lashed back with his foot, kicking at Owen. But as the smoke cleared, all that could be seen was Medwick lying on his back atop the base kicking at the hometown favorite.

Figuring that there must be something in the Geneva Convention outlawing such doings, the Tigers fans finally had something to get worked up over. And when Medwick went out to take his place in left field in the bottom of the sixth, he was greeted by 18,000 fans in the wooden bleachers, who rained a thunderstorm of trash on the field, including lemons, tomatoes, and heads of lettuce. Four times Medwick was called off the field, only to reassume his position and ignite an even higher crescendo of frustration and hate from the Tigers' fans. Finally, after twenty minutes of watching the greengrocers in the bleachers fling their wares in Medwick's direction, baseball commissioner Kenesaw Mountain Landis had had enough. Summoning Medwick and his manager, Frankie Frisch, over to his box, Landis excused Medwick for the rest of the game. Afterward Medwick was to say, "I knew why they threw it at me. What I can't figure out is why they brought it to the ballpark in the first place."

Dizzy Dean, who had led the rip-snorting "Gashouse Gang" to the 1934 National League pennant with his thirty wins, prided himself on his batting and baserunning more than his pitching. And so, after pitching the Cardinals to victory in the opener of the '34 Series, Dizzy sat, none too quietly, on the bench watching the rest of the proceedings for the next two games. Finally, in game four, Dizzy had had enough of not enough and inserted himself into the game as a pinch runner in the fourth inning. Roaring into second to break up a double play, Dean forgot to slide and took Detroit shortstop Billy Rogell's throw to first right between the eyes. He tottered, swayed, and after a brief pause came down like a felled oak under the woodman's ax. Carried off the field semiconscious, Dean was rushed to a nearby St. Louis hospital for X rays. After being released, Dean held one of his ad hoc press conferences and told the concert assembled, "The doctors X rayed my head and didn't find anything."

John Leonard Roosevelt "Pepper" Martin had just put on the greatest one-man show in the history of the World Series: twelve hits in eighteen at-bats, five runs scored, seven runs batted in, and four bases stolen. Single-handedly he had brought the 1931 St. Louis Cardinals to the brink of victory and was the toast of the country. As the team pushed its way through the throngs at Philadelphia's Broad Street Station for their trip back to St. Louis where they would clinch the world championship, baseball commissioner Kenesaw Mountain Landis, as caught up in the drama as any ordinary fan, sought out the hero and proclaimed, "Young man, I'd like to be in your place tonight." Letting the remark set in, Pepper grinned and retorted, "Well, Judge, tell you what . . .

I'll swap places. And salaries. My $4,500 for your $65,000."
Proving that like others, he knew that ballplayers during the
Great Depression were born and not paid.

Old Jack Quinn, or more properly, John Picus Quinn, was
still pitching in 1930, well into his forty-seventh year, his
twenty-second as a major league pitcher. After he had become the oldest player in the history of the World Series,
pitching two innings in the 1930 classic, a reporter came up
to him and asked him why he was pitching after all these
years. Quinn looked at the peach-fuzz in front of him and
answered, curtly: "One wife and six kids."

Babe Ruth was famous for not remembering names. He
had nicknames for all players, names like Chicken Neck, Flop
Ears, Duck Eye, Horse Nose, Rubber Belly, and other
noncomplimentary appellations, which he used mainly because he couldn't remember their given names. When Waite
Hoyt was traded by the Yankees to the Detroit Tigers
midway through the 1930 season, Ruth solemnly shook hands
with the man who had been his teammate for more than nine
years and said, "Well, good-bye, Walter."

Red Smith tells of the time the then king of sportswriters,
Grantland Rice, had Babe Ruth on his weekly radio show.
Given a script with prearranged questions and answers, Ruth
answered one of Rice's questions with a "Well, you know,

Granny, Duke Ellington said the Battle of Waterloo was won on the playing fields of Elkton." Afterwards, the more-than-somewhat-bemused Rice could only say, "Duke Ellington for the Duke of Wellington, I can understand. But how did you ever read Eton as Elkton? That's in Maryland, isn't it?" Ruth looked at Rice and explained, "I married my first wife there, and I always hated the goddamn place."

Zeke Bonura's bat was a lethal weapon. So, too, was his glove, when he deigned to wave it at a passing ball in what became known as the "Mussolini Salute." Called "the Banana King"—as much for his family's business in New Orleans as for his schnozz—Bonura was quirky. He once drove from Washington to Chicago to get back home to New Orleans after the White Sox had traded him to the Senators—that being the only way he knew.

He played first in much the same roundabout manner, but always enthusiastically, pounding his glove and shouting encouragement no matter what the situation. One time, with the bases loaded and two out, the batter dribbled a ball in Bonura's direction. Zeke pounced on the ball and picked it up, but the ball failed to cooperate and popped out of his glove. Bonura scooped it up again, and once more it dropped out. Then he managed to kick it around a little, giving an impersonation of Charlie Chaplin trying to pick up his hat. By the time Bonura had finally found the handle and managed to pick up the ball, all three base runners had crossed the plate and the batter was heading toward third. Zeke took a bead on third and promptly fired the ball into the opposing dugout, allowing the man who had hit the dribbler to score with the fourth run—all on what should have been the third out of the inning.

As soon as the fourth run had scored, Bonura pounded his glove and shouted to the pitcher, "Thataway, stick in there, kid. We'll win this one for you!"

Burleigh Grimes was, among other things, an anachronism. For the man who was the last of the (legal) spitball pitchers was also a throwback to the good old days, when bench jockeying and baiting recalled the worst excesses of the French Revolution. Called "Ol' Stubblebeard" for his perpetual five-o'clock shadow, Grimes was as black of heart as he was of beard, using his tongue as well as his spitball.

But by 1932 he was at the end of his long career, working as a spot pitcher for the Chicago Cubs. On the day in question he was on the mound when rookie third baseman Stan Hack kicked away a ground ball and snapped his fingers in disgust, prompting Grimes to hurl some choice epithets in the general direction of third. Two more men reached base against Grimes, loading them up. Then, with two out, Hack booted another grounder, and again snapped his fingers in disgust. This time there wasn't even time to scowl before manager Rogers Hornsby gave Grimes a free pass to the shower. Grimes was furious. "Why take me out?" he yelled. (Here we take a time-out to allow our readers to insert their favorite four-letter words.) "Why not take out that guy who's only snapping his fingers at the ball?"

Denton True Young—better known as "Cy," as in "Cyclone"—was baseball's first truly great pitcher, hurling for twenty-two years on both sides of the twentieth-century divide. During that spell, Young won 511 games, pitched 751 complete games, and had five thirty-game and sixteen twenty-game seasons. His greatness was recognized when, in the second year of Hall of Fame voting, he was elected to Cooperstown. And so it was that Young appeared at the first Hall of Fame inductions in 1939, along with other such greats as Ruth, Cobb, Johnson, and Wagner, and mingled with the crowd of fans and sportswriters. One young sportswriter, seeing an opportunity for a big story, rushed up to the side of the seventy-two-year-old ancient and began filling the air with questions. After bombarding Young for a while, the pencil-pusher asked, "What was your favorite pitch when the opponents loaded the bases?" "My boy," Young said, "I can't recollect ever having to pitch with the bases full." As Young turned to leave, the young writer tried one more time. "One more question, sir," he pleaded. Young stopped. "How many games did you win, Mr. Young," he asked, showing that he didn't know enough to know he knew but little. Young, realizing he was dealing with someone mentally unarmed, merely answered, "Young man, I won more games than you'll ever see," and walked away.

As a manager, Rogers Hornsby was a strict disciplinarian, one who would countenance no deviation from his orders. As the pilot of the lowly St. Louis Browns, Hornsby always seemed to be posting more orders than wins. Still, this martinet demanded that they be followed to the letter. One rule was that pitchers with a count of two strikes and no balls must waste a pitch; failure to do so would result in a fifty-dollar fine. As fate would have it, one afternoon during the 1935 season, pitcher Jim Walkup got to an 0–2 count on the batter and threw one he thought was a little outside the strike zone. But the umpire saw it differently, ruling that it had nicked the corner, and jerked up his right hand to indicate "Strike three!" Walkup, facing the fine for violating one of Hornsby's edicts, rushed the plate and pleaded with the umpire to reverse his call. But the call stuck. And so did the fifty-dollar fine.

When Rogers Hornsby took over as manager of the godawful St. Louis Browns at the end of the 1933 season he inherited a pitching staff with arms up for adoption. The ace of the staff—an oxymoron for a pitcher with nineteen losses and an ERA of 4.72—was one George Blaeholder. Hornsby decided that Blaeholder was his personal reclamation project for '34, and so, before every start, Hornsby painstakingly went over the opposing batting order with him. One of those he singled out for Blaeholder's attention was Doc Cramer, one of the best hitters on the Philadelphia Athletics, who, not incidentally, seemed to own Blaeholder. But try as Hornsby might, nothing he said seemed to sink in, and Cramer continued to fatten up his batting average at Blaeholder's expense.

One afternoon Cramer hit a clean-up home run off Blaeholder, the blow struck, Hornsby quickly detected, off a "wrong" pitch. With his instructions so openly flouted, Hornsby quickly confronted Blaeholder and vented his sulfuric spleen—along with every four-letter word at his command. At the end of five minutes of nonstop vitriol Hornsby finally sneered, "I don't believe you even know who you were pitching to, do you, Blaeholder?" The pitcher scratched his head, shuffled his feet, and mumbled, "I'll think of it in a minute, Skip. . . . It's right here on the tip of my tongue." That was enough for Hornsby, struck dumb by his equally dumb pitcher. By the beginning of the next year Hornsby had shuffled Blaeholder off to Philadelphia, where he joined his old nemesis, Cramer, on the A's.

Some managers, it has been said, manage by the seat of their pants; Ossie Vitt could be said to have managed by the skin of his teeth. Literally. Seems that when Vitt—who managed the 1937 Newark Bears, called by many the greatest team in minor league history for winning the International League pennant by an unbelievable twenty-five-and-a-half games—took over the reigns of the 1938 Cleveland Indians, he brought with him not only his hard-driving tactics, but also a case of bad teeth. What with getting acquainted with the personnel on his new club and trying to keep the front-running Yankees in his sights, Vitt never found time to go to the dentist. And so it was that for the first six weeks of the season Vitt suffered from both his teeth and the aforementioned Yankees. When Yankee manager Joe McCarthy heard of Vitt's plight, he wasn't too sympathetic toward his lodge brother. "Suffering with a toothache, eh?" repeated the hard-as-nails McCarthy. "Well, why doesn't he go and have them pulled? He pulls his pitchers when they're going bad, doesn't he?"

Casey Stengel once said of Vince DiMaggio, "Vince is the only player I ever saw who could strike out three times in one game and not be embarrassed. He'd walk into the clubhouse whistling. Everybody would be feeling sorry for him, but Vince always thought he was doing good." The elder DiMaggio brother's premiere season in the big leagues for Stengel and the Boston Braves was 1937. And right from the start, he was striking out a lot—he led the league in strikeouts his very first year—and whistling a lot. Another who was whistling that year—until a line shot by Earl Averill in the 1937 All-Star Game cut short his pitching career—was St. Louis Cardinal right-hander Dizzy Dean, whose whistling fast ball had enabled him to lead the league in strikeouts in four of the previous five years.

On the afternoon in question, Vince had faced Dizzy's smoke and come up second best, striking out twice. In the ninth inning, Vince came to bat again. After taking two called strikes, he managed to get his ash around on a third Dean smoker and lifted a pop foul of less than epic proportions behind the plate. Dean ran in and screamed to the catcher, "Let her drop! Don't catch it!" The catcher, distracted by Dean's screams, let the ball drop, unmolested. At that point St. Louis manager Frankie Frisch came storming out of the dugout. "What's the big idea?" he shouted at Dean. The nonplussed Dean looked at Frisch with something that resembled pity for someone who didn't see his logic, said, "unnerstan'," and tried to explain: "I bet ten bucks I'd fan DiMaggio three times today . . . and this is my last chance." And with that, as Frisch stood stock still, his mouth moving but no words coming out, Dean turned back to the mound. And to the business at hand, which he finished on the next pitch. Old Diz struck out Vince for the third time to win his bet.

Walter Beck was known familiarly by his nickname, "Boom-Boom." How he came by that moniker is a story unto itself, one that is among baseball's favorite thrice-told tales and bears retelling. It seems that Beck was playing for the old-old Brooklyn Dodgers, the team that had managed to amass the greatest number of clowns in baseball uniforms ever assembled under one tent. Chief among them was Lewis Robert Wilson, a.k.a. "Hack." Wilson, whose five-foot-six body would bear strict inspection, and gave him his nickname, a shortened version of the name of a wrestler, Hackenschmidt, was one of the greatest hitters of the early 1930s. But in that double-entry bookkeeping that tallies all of baseball's debits and credits as precisely as an accountant's ledger, Wilson's deficiencies in the field left his account sorely in the red. His after-hour tippling usually left his face and nose in the red as well.

One June day in 1934, Wilson, who believed that being a good liver was infinitely better than having one, was desperately hung over after a rough night out on the town. The town in question was Philadelphia, and the ballpark postage-stamp-sized Baker Bowl, where the right-field tin wall was just a stone's throw from home plate. With Beck pitching and the Phillies hitting, the right-field wall had doubled as a handball wall, several hits having cascaded off in the vicinity of Wilson, who had spent most of his energy running them down. Finally, Brooklyn manager Casey Stengel had had enough, and marched out to the mound to give the pitcher a free pass to the showers. But Beck was having none of it. Asked for the ball by Stengel, Beck instead wheeled around and threw the ball as hard as he could. The ball, taking flight like everything else that afternoon, hit the right-field fence, hard by the infield. And hard by Wilson's head, which at that moment was between his legs, a vestigial reminder of the indiscretions of the night before. The drowsing Wilson, crouched over in his what-the-hell-let's-go-fishing posture, hands on knees, head down, was aroused by the clatter of the ball banging off the tin barrier. Leaping to his task faster than anyone could say "John Barleycorn," Wilson fielded the ball and fired a perfect strike into second. The play, one of the last made by Wilson in his major league career, forever branded Beck with the name "Boom-Boom," the sound of the ball rattling off the Baker Bowl fence.

But the story doesn't end there. After Wilson's throw to second baseman Tony Cuccinello—"A helluva throw, the best he's made all year," Cuccinello was to say later—Stengel spied Beck kicking buckets in the dugout. "Cut that out!" Stengel bellowed. "You'll break a toe and I won't be able to get anything for you." And by the end of the year, both Beck and Wilson were gone.

The Brooklyn Dodgers were always the "Toys Я Us" franchise of baseball. Coming on the heels of the "Daffiness Boys" of the 1920s were the clowns of the '30s, managed, of course, by Casey Stengel, who could almost have cornered the market by himself. But even Casey was nearly driven sane by the antics of his flock. One of those entrusted to Casey's care was Stanley "Frenchy" Bordagaray, a free-spirited outfielder who wore a mustache "just to be different"—and was, in caps. In a close game during the 1935 season, Bordagaray found himself on second—momentarily. Or at least until he was picked off, breaking up a promising rally. When he returned to the bench, Stengel exploded in a torrent of four-letter expletives, demanding, "What happened?" "Gee, Case, I don't know," replied Bordagaray, sounding like a little boy minimizing a bad school report. "I was standing out there, tapping the base with my foot, and I guess I got caught somewhere between the taps."

Casey Stengel was not always blessed, as when he was the Yankee manager, with an abundance of talent. In fact, if the truth be known, there were times his talent was so theadbare it could have been sent out for reupholstering. Such was the case when Casey was manager of the Brooklyn Dodgers in the mid-1930s and numbered among his charges the likes of Frenchy Bordagaray, Van Lingle Mungo, and others destined to spend their lives in the environs of the second division.

One afternoon Stengel was in the third-base coaching box at the Polo Grounds in a close game against the Dodgers' perennial rivals, the New York Giants, when infielder Tony Cuccinello drove a hit to the bullpen in far right field. Giant outfielder Mel Ott fielded the ball cleanly on one hop and drilled a throw to third base just as Cuccinello came into the base. "Slide! Slide!" screamed the excitable Stengel, but Cuccinello came into the base standing up and was tagged out by third baseman Travis Jackson. Stengel, beside himself, shouted at Cuccinello, "I told you to slide. You'd have been safe a mile! Why didn't you slide when I told you to?" "Slide?" repeated Cuccinello, with dignity drawing himself up to his full height, "and bust my cigars?"

In a day and age when an Italian ballplayer was a rarity, the New York Yankees of the late 1930s had seemingly cornered the market, having such stars as Joe DiMaggio, Frankie Crosetti, and Tony Lazzeri on their roster. Proud of their heritage and prouder still of their accomplishments, the three formed a tight little group, addressing each other good-naturedly as "Big Dago," "Little Dago," and plain ol' "Dago." The only other player allowed admission to their tight little clique was baseball's reigning imp, pitcher Lefty Gomez, who was entitled to all the privileges of name-calling and poking fun at them or at himself. Gomez, who roomed with DiMaggio, was often heard to say, "They didn't know DiMaggio could go back on a ball until he played behind me."

All four once played a part in a sequence that hinged on their closeness. Seems that on the afternoon in question, Gomez was pitching and had just picked up a sacrifice bunt hit back toward the mound. As DiMaggio came in from center field to back up second, Lazzeri moved from second to cover first and Crosetti moved from short to cover second. Gomez wheeled and threw the ball to a surprised DiMaggio, who was in no position to make a play anywhere.

After the inning was over, Yankee manager Joe McCarthy, more than a little perturbed at the goings-on, approached Gomez, and between words that would cause paint to peel off walls, demanded, "What happened?" Without batting an eye, Gomez answered, "Geez, they were all hollering, 'Throw it to the Dago,' but they didn't say which Dago." Momentarily rendered speechless, all McCarthy could do was harrumph and mutter, "From now on, identify which Dago."

During the Depression Babe Ruth was asked to take a reduction in his already healthy salary, but held out for $80,000. When a club official protested, "But that's more money than Herbert Hoover got for being president last year," the Babe answered, "I know, but I had a better year."

Lefty Gomez was one of baseball's reigning pitchers and reigning wits for the better part of ten years. One year, after being asked to take a salary cut—as much the result of a poor season as the effect of the Depression—from $20,000 to $7,500, the shocked Gomez told Yankee general manager Ed Barrow, "Tell you what, you keep the salary and pay me the cut."

The Yankees of the late 1930s were alternately called "Murderers' Row" and "the Window Breakers," testimony to their ability to score at will and win about as frequently— they led the American League in both scoring and wins for four straight years, 1936 through 1939. Their mound ace during those four years was a grizzled right-hander named "Red" Ruffing. Ruffing had back-to-back-to-back-to-back years of twenty, twenty, twenty-one, and twenty-one wins. Yet his ERA was hardly as sterling, since he was given to letting up when he had a big lead. One who noted Ruffing's lack of concentration with a lead was Yankee shortstop Frankie Crosetti, who would always tell Ruffing before he pitched, "I hope we don't get you a lot of runs, because all you'll do is be a Thomas Edison out there—experimenting."

For twelve years Tony Lazzeri was the unsung hero of some of the greatest Yankee teams of all time, the man who supplied the ballast to clubs filled with enough prima donnas to start an opera company. Time and again the man the fans lovingly called "Poosh 'Em Up Tony" would take charge when trouble threatened. And so it was one afternoon that, after the great Yankee left-hander Vernon "Lefty" Gomez had filled the bases on three walks, Lazzeri came trotting in from second to talk to his knight errant. Fully expecting to be assuaged or to hear some words of wisdom that would turn the situation around, Gomez turned to hear out Lazzeri. All he heard was, "You put those runners on there. Now get out of the jam yourself, you slob."

Smead Jolley was at one with his bat, but his fielding was hardly a contribution to the arts. During his four years in the majors in the early 1930s, Jolley hit .300 or better four times. Unfortunately, his fielding average was only slightly higher, and it became a problem to find him a place in the field where he wouldn't destroy his team. Finally, after two years, the Chicago White Sox gave up on him and sent him to the Boston Red Sox.

Unfortunately, Fenway Park at that time featured an incline leading to the wall known as "Duffy's Cliff," after Duffy Lewis, who had successfully conquered the slope when he was part of baseball's greatest outfield, alongside Tris Speaker and Harry Hooper. Jolley, however, was no Lewis and needed coaching on how to negotiate the hill. Red Sox coach Eddie Collins worked with Jolley, showing him how to run back under a fly ball and take the hill in stride. Finally, Boston manager Marty McManus thought it was safe to entrust Jolley with left field. And vice versa. But in his first game Jolley ran back for a well-hit ball and then, realizing he had overrun it, came forward again, down the incline, and fell flat on his face. The ball hit him on the head and bounded merrily away. After the inning had mercifully came to an end, Jolley returned to the dugout rubbing his head and, creasing his three chins into six or seven, complained, "Ten days you guys spend teaching me how to go up the hill and there isn't one of you with the brains to teach me how to come down again."

Ty Cobb was a proud, fiercely competitive man whose volcanic emotions lay just beneath the surface, ready to erupt at the slightest tremor. One of the tremors that constantly ignited Cobb was any questioning of his abilities, especially when his talents were compared to those of latter-day players. And so it was that when Cobb appeared at the 1939 World's Fair in Flushing Meadows and a reporter asked him how he'd do against modern pitching. Cobb, without batting the proverbial lash, answered, "I'd probably hit about .320, maybe .325." The reporter swallowed hard and asked the next obvious question: "But Mr. Cobb, your lifetime average was .367 and you've always said you felt the pitchers of today weren't as good as those you faced. Why," he went on, "do you think you'd only hit .320 now?" "You've got to remember something, sonny," the irascible Cobb snapped. "I'm fifty-two years old now!"

Gabby Hartnett was a rosy-cheeked catcher who lived up to his nickname. But one time even "the Gabby One" was dumbstruck. Hartnett was working with a rookie pitcher for the Cubs, about to make his first start. After going through the signals in the clubhouse before the game, Hartnett came out to the mound and handed the youngster the ball, along with some instructions. "Listen kid, I'll flash one finger for a fast ball, two for a curve, and three for a change of pace. Got that? Alright, let's go!"

With that, Hartnett took his place behind the batter, squatted on his hunkies, and signaled for a fast ball. The rookie nodded his assent, wound up, and let the ball fly—all the way to the backstop for a wild pitch. Hartnett sighed, got back down in his crouch, and once again signaled for the fast pitch, shooting out one finger. This pitch hit the dirt ten feet in front of the plate and exited to the dugout. Hartnett called for time and walked out to the mound. "Listen, kid," he intoned, "there's nothing to be nervous about—"

"I'm not nervous, Gabby," the rookie cut in. "It's just that I can't seem to throw a fast ball with one finger. . . . "

In one of those bull sessions that often break out around baseball's campfires and cracker barrels, the subject had turned to relief pitching. The bull-sessioners mentioned such

The Thirties

names as Wilcy Moore, Firpo Marberry, Johnny Murphy, Hugh Casey, and the latest relief star, Joe Page of the Yankees. One of those in the session turned to Lefty Gomez, the great Yankee southpaw of another day, and asked El Goofy, "What do you think, Lefty? Who would you rate the greater reliever, Page or Murphy?" Gomez smiled and thought a bit. Finally, he said, "I couldn't be a fair judge of that. I've watched Page a number of times. But I can't give an opinion of Murphy. I never did get to see that guy pitch." "Never saw him pitch?" asked one of the puzzled members of the bull session. "Why, you were on the same team with him for years!" "Yeah," came back Lefty, "but every time he was working, I was taking a shower."

The
Forties

Allie Reynolds counted 182 wins and one home run among his lifetime accomplishments. That one home run came in the opening game of the 1948 season against Washington Senators pitcher Early Wynn. Reynolds would have gone into his home-run trot, except he didn't know how, so he ran all the way. When he galloped by second he looked up and "saw the third base coach holding up his hands." Thinking the coach meant for him to go back, Reynolds slid back into second. "It was pretty embarrassing, especially since it was opening day and the President of the United States was in the stands," remembers Reynolds about his singular feat.

During World War II, baseball scouts combed the country signing babes in swaddling clothes and throwing mosquito nets over anybody this side of Civil War veterans. In fact, everyone but the Singer Midgets had been conscripted for what had been the national pastime before the war supplanted it—and rumors were bruited about that four or five teams were attempting to sign even them to contracts. By the time the 1945 World Series rolled around, most of the major leaguers were still awaiting their marching orders, so the Detroit Tigers and the Chicago Cubs were forced to make do with teams that couldn't have bought their way in during more peaceful times. Before the Series started, a poll of sportswriters found that forty-five of the eighty favored the Tigers over the Cubs. The only writer abstaining from the vote was Chicago scribe Warren Brown who, suspecting that there was not enough caffeine in the world to keep him awake during the upcoming World Series, said, "I've seen 'em both play and I don't think either team can win it."

The fans in Boston had their own DiMaggio, Dominic, whom they celebrated in a takeoff on Wagner's opera *Tann-häuser* as "Faster than his brother, Joe, Dom-in-ic Di-Maggio." Others were also ready to grant that younger brother Dominic was a better fielder than Joe, including Joe himself. During one of those crucial Red Sox–Yankee series in the late 1940s that always seemed to decide the American League pennant winner, Dom turned his toes to pasture and, running in a smooth, unbroken line, managed to catch a drive by Joe that no one but a DiMaggio could ever have reached, let alone caught. Sitting in the press box, writer Sid Mercer remarked to one and all, "Joe should sue his old man on that one." After the game Joe would add, "The kid didn't have to rub it in that way . . . Especially when he's coming to my house for dinner tonight."

Many of the so-called Boys of Summer were given their "Days" at Ebbets Field in the late 1940s. One such "Day" was given to local Brooklyn boy Hank Behrman, a "herky-jerky" relief pitcher who won twenty-one games and saved nineteen more for the Dodgers from 1946 to 1948. Behrman was one of those who would more than occasionally tarry at life's tavern, tipping "a cup of kindness for auld lang syne." So it was only fitting that his friends placed little boxes on the bar in neighborhood saloons to raise funds for a gift to be presented to him on Hank Behrman Day.

On the day of the presentation, a fan came out of the stands and gave Behrman an envelope. He gravely intoned, "Hank Behrman, your friends and neighbors want to pay tribute to you . . ." Behrman suspiciously looked at the envelope and said, "What's in it?" The presenter, momentarily taken aback, could only reply, "A $100 savings bond." "Fer Christ sakes," said the by-now infuriated Behrman. "Campanella got a car, Roe gets a cabin cruiser, and all I get is a $100 bond? Shove it up your ass!" And with that, he threw the envelope down on home plate and walked away, showing none of the appreciation Yogi Berra would show at his "Day," when he thanked everyone "for making this day necessary." Up in the press box, writer Tom Meany, knowing Behrman had potential paternity problems, was heard to mutter, "He's lucky it's not a subpoena."

RAIN DELAYS

Remember that towering fly ball struck by Roy Hobbs with his trusty bat "Wonder Boy" that broke the scoreboard clock to smithereens in the movie *The Natural*? Well, it happened in real life just as it did in reel life. For author Bernard Malamud, never wandering too far afield from fact, based his protagonist, Roy Hobbs, on the past exploits of several players, including, but not limited to, Joe Jackson, Eddie Waitkus, Billy Jurges, and Corvel "Bama" Rowell. It was the last-named of this real-life quartet, Bama Rowell, who, while playing for the 1946 edition of the Boston Braves, hit a towering fly ball toward the Ebbets Field right-field fence—more specifically, toward the huge Bulova clock that stood majestically atop the scoreboard. Just like its cinematic counterpart some three-and-a-half decades later, the ball struck the clock, shattering it into little pieces—or, as Malamud wrote, "The clock spattered minutes all over the place,"—and showered Dodger right fielder Dixie Walker with falling glass.

Bama Rowell was tracked down forty-one years later by the author at his home in Citronelle, Alabama, where he tried to recall the specifics of what he called "a high fly ball." "I don't remember exactly when it was, but I do know it was four-twenty in the afternoon, 'cause the clock broke." (Actually, according to a contemporary account of the previous day's game in the May 31, 1946, edition of *The New York Times*, it happened at 4:25 and the clock didn't stop until an hour later.) Rowell remembered one other thing: "Anyone hitting the Bulova clock was supposed to get a free watch, but I never did get no watch yet."

Postscript: After hearing of Rowell's plaint, Bulova was forced to spring for that watch, forty-one years late—another example of time standing still.

Major league baseball and radio became an "item" when Gillette signed a long-term contract to sponsor the 1939 World Series. In the early '40s Gillette added a little fillip, getting participants in each Series to give their personal endorsements for the Gillette Safety Razor. When St. Louis Cardinal manager Billy Southworth was asked by the staff announcer whether he had shaved with a Gillette razor that morning, Southworth answered in the affirmative: "You know bloody well I did!"

Back in 1942 a home run by the Milwaukee Brewers of the American Association was never merely a home run. It was a "Wheaties Wallop"—just as it was a "Ballantine Blast" in New York, an "Old Goldie" in Brooklyn, and a "Chesterfield Satisfier" in Washington. During that year General Mills purchased a portion of the Brewers' radio broadcasts to extend its Breakfast of Champions franchise beyond its postpubescent Jack Armstrong image. The team hit more home runs that year than any team in the majors, with the notable exceptions of the Yankees and the Giants. And General Mills celebrated each and every "Wheaties Wallop" with a free case of the breakfast food. The first case of twenty-four boxes was always taken home to feed the player's family. After that, however, the players would let them stack up in owner Bill Veeck's office. As the home run total grew, so did the stack of cases, higher and higher. Finally, at the end of the season, Veeck decided to take some to his farm in West Bend, Wisconsin. He transported almost sixty cases home in a pickup truck and threw the boxes into the pigpen near the farmhouse. The next morning he came out to view a scene that resembled a conveyor belt run amok. Seems the pigs had eaten the boxes. And the glassine overwraps. But they had left untouched the Breakfast of Champions.

For years Gladys Goodding was the organist at Ebbets Field in Brooklyn, providing between-innings songs and sometimes even putting into song what the Dodger faithful were screaming from the stands. "Goodding" is the answer to one of the oldest trivia questions, one with a decided curve—"Who was the only person ever to play for the Knicks, Rangers, and Dodgers in the same year?" She won her job at Ebbets Field after having played the organ at Madison Square Garden for years at Knick and Ranger games. Umpire Bill Stewart, who doubled in brass as a hockey referee during the off season, knew Gladys and her work. As Stewart and his two fellow umpires, Ziggy Sears and Tom Dunn, were about to walk out onto the field for a day game on May 9, 1942, Stewart was explaining that she was a friend of his. No sooner had the three umpires stepped onto the field than Goodding welcomed them with "Three Blind Mice," causing Sears and Dunn to glower at Stewart and say, "I thought you said she was a friend of yours!"

What the Chicago Cubs' lilliputian outfielder Dom Dallessandro lacked in stature, he more than made up in feistiness. One hot summer afternoon in the early 1940s, the Cub outfielder was called out on strikes by umpire George Magerkurth on a borderline call. Dallessandro couldn't believe the call, and told Magerkurth, a hulking six-foot-three mountain of a man, exactly what he thought of his eyesight. And parentage. Magerkurth had had just about enough of Dallessandro's jumping up and down, and finally grunted in his general direction, "Listen, you little runt, if you don't shut up, I'll bite your head off." "If you do," Dallessandro shouted at the man-mountain in front of him, "you'll have more brains in your big belly than you have in your head."

In 1946 the Yankees brought up two youngsters for a late-season look-see: Larry Berra—later to become familiarly known as "Yogi"—and Bobby Brown. Both were to play in seven games, show great promise, and be brought up to stay in '47. And stay with each other as roommates in one of the oddest pairings this side of Neil Simon. Brown, a premed student, took to toting around his heavy medical tomes on road trips. Berra found comic books made for lighter carrying—and reading. One night, by coincidence, both finished their reading at exactly the same moment. As Yogi turned the last page of his thirty-two-page comic book he looked over at Brown, who had just put down his massive copy of *Gray's Anatomy*, and with a slight interest, tinged with faint bewilderment, said, "Mine was great. How'd yours come out?"

Ewell Blackwell was known as "the Whip." And with good reason. He was so thin that he looked like he worked in an olive factory, dragging the pimento through. Blackwell came at the batter by way of third base, whipping the ball in sidearmed. In 1947 Blackwell led the National League in wins, complete games, and strikeouts. Although he never finished near the league leaders in wins or complete games again after a kidney infection in '48, year after year Blackwell was still a threat to strike out any batter he faced—even Stan Musial. And so it was that during a game between the Cincinnati Reds and the St. Louis Cardinals in 1949, Blackwell threw a sizzler by Musial, striking out "the Man." Unfortunately, he threw it by catcher Dixie Howell as well, allowing Musial to go all the way to second on the strikeout. In the Reds' dugout, manager Bucky Walters threw his cap on the ground and was heard to mutter, "That guy Musial is so good that even when he fans you're lucky to hold him to two bases."

Ted Lyons had been pitching for the Chicago White Sox for what seemed like forever. Actually it was only since he had come off the Baylor University campus in 1923. In 1942 he was a "Sunday pitcher," pitching every Sunday, and compiling the enviable tally of twenty games started, twenty games completed, and a fourteen-and-six record, the most wins on the Sox staff.

Lyons joined the Navy in '43, and his next pitching position was with a service club on Guam. And what to his wondering eyes should appear in his very first game but an army outfit starring Joe DiMaggio. Lyons, who remembered only too well that DiMaggio had hit him like he owned him— even connecting twice against him to extend his fifty-six-game hit streak—let out an audible groan upon seeing DiMag. "I left the country to get away from DiMaggio," Lyons said aloud, "and here he is!"

The winds of war gusted over America in 1941 and everybody, athletes included, was caught up in the ensuing draft. One of those drafted was pitcher Kirby Higbe, who had led the National League in wins and his beloved Dodgers to the National League pennant in 1941. Higbe served his time overseas, where he made the acquaintance of a nurse. After Higbe's return to the states, she wrote him a letter care of the Dodgers, salting it with endearments and scenting it with perfume. Unfortunately for Higbe, the Dodgers, as was their custom, forwarded the letter to his home, where Mrs. Higbe intercepted it. "What's this?" Mrs. Higbe demanded of her husband. Thinking quickly, Kirby answered, "Oh, that's not for me. That's for someone else named Kirby Higbe."

Toots Shor was the owner-proprietor of New York's most famous watering hole during the 1940s and '50s, a place where sports stars congregated, particularly the New York Giants, Shor's favorites. One evening Shor was talking to Sir Alexander Fleming, the discoverer of penicillin, when a waiter sidled up to Shor's elbow with the news that Giants' manager, Mel Ott, had just arrived. "Excuse me," said Shor to Fleming, putting his perspectives in order, "but I gotta leave. Somebody important just came in."

One night Joe DiMaggio was seated at a front table at Toots Shor's explaining to one and all how he justified his holdout for $75,000. Joe D's arguing points included that a player's peak activity is limited to just a few years, that he's constantly fighting the inroads of encroaching age, and that he must make use of his limited time. One of those congregated around the table listening to DiMaggio was Mrs. Paul Gallico, the wife of the famed sportswriter. "Now," spoke up Mrs. Gallico, without sympathy, "you have some idea of how it feels to be a woman."

Dick Wakefield was one of baseball's early bonus busts. Before World War II his bat had been compared to that of batting leader Ted Williams; after he returned from the war it was compared to bandleader Ted Weem's baton. On one occasion manager Steve O'Neill of the Detroit Tigers was cornered by members of the out-of-town press corps who wanted to know more about Wakefield and why he had suddenly come up short. "What's the story on this guy?" asked one of the dandruff-scratchers. "Well," O'Neill led off, accompanying his words with a shake of the head, "Wakefield is built for slugging. Right now he's in perfect shape. He has great form at the plate. He takes a pretty cut at the ball. In fact, there's only one thing lacking." "What's that?" they said, almost in unison. "He just can't hit it," said O'Neill of his less-than-tigerish Tiger.

Immediately after World War II, Joe Medwick, the former St. Louis Cardinal outfielder, visited the Vatican along with a group who had been granted an audience. As each visitor approached him the Pope asked him his vocation. When Medwick's turn came he stepped forward and said to the pontiff, "Your Holiness, I'm Joseph Medwick, and I used to be a Cardinal."

On the day his noble experiment as baseball's first black was to begin, Jackie Robinson kissed his wife Rachel goodbye at their hotel and said, "Honey, if you come out to Ebbets Field today you won't have any trouble recognizing me. . . . " And then, with the timing and skill of a Jack Benny, he added, "My number is forty-two."

Lou Novikoff was one of those minor league phenoms who somehow, someway, never quite make it in the big leagues. A member of the Softball Hall of Fame who turned his attentions to hard ball, Novikoff burned up the minors in his first four-plus years of professional ball, batting .365 overall and leading several leagues, including the Pacific Coast League, in batting.

Called up by the Chicago Cubs in 1941, Novikoff never acquitted his buildup. Maybe it was the curve ball, as some claim; maybe it was his makeup, which earned him the name "the Mad Russian." But while he was in the majors, he left his mark, if not for his ball-playing, then for his madcap antics. On one afternoon he brought tears to the eyes of manager Charlie Grimm. And not tears of joy either. For, with the bases loaded, Novikoff took off from second and slid into third, there to be tagged for the rally-ending third out. Confronting his errant knight in the dugout, Grimm demanded an explanation of what made Louie run. And Lou had an explanation: "I couldn't resist, Charlie. I never had a better jump on the pitcher."

By 1942 every able-bodied Johnny, Teddy, and Bobby had gone marching off to war. For the next four years the sixteen teams in the majors stocked their rosters with men who would have done Emma Lazarus proud—the wrong, the short, and the nearly blind; in short, the 4F-ers. Scouts were combing the country as baseball took on the look of a giant mission. The Senators signed a former sanitation worker; the Dodgers brought back Babe Herman after a seven-year absence, only to see him fall over first on his first base hit; and the Browns signed the most famous of all the wartime players, one-armed Pete Gray.

One of the players signed by the Brooklyn Dodgers was a sixteen-year-old hometown boy, Tommy Brown. In those days tobacco companies were the principal advertiser of baseball games, and the Dodgers had arranged with the manufacturers of Old Gold cigarettes to give away a carton of P. Lorillard's finest to any Dodger who hit a home run; the carton was to be sent careening down the screen behind the plate after the homer. On the occasion of Brown's first major league home run—August 20, 1945—the flunky in the Ebbets Field press box dutifully sent the carton sliding down the screen in the direction of the youth, only to see Brooklyn manager Leo Durocher grab it before Brown could reach it. As Durocher intercepted the carton he turned to Brown and told his fuzzy-cheeked charge, "You're too young to smoke these." With that he confiscated the week's supply of free smokes for himself.

Little Kenny Smith was a proud sportswriter, one who stood tall in his profession despite the fact that one sportswriter called him "Walking Short." Through his many years of writing baseball for the New York *Mirror*—a tabloid that was charitably third in a two-tabloid town—Smith had seen it all. Or thought he had. One of the things Smith had seen was the expansion of the playing of "The Star-Spangled Banner" from one time a year, opening day, to every day during World War II. But with the coming of peace and the restoration of normalcy, "The Star-Spangled Banner" continued to be played before each game. Finally tiring of the packaged patriotism, Smith, after one particularly tiring rendition of Francis Scott Key's adaptation of the English drinking ballad, muttered aloud to anyone who could hear him in the press box, "Does Macy's play 'The Star-Spangled Banner' every day before they open their damned doors?"

One of those apocryphal stories that became attached to Franklin Delano Roosevelt had him making a call to Joseph Stalin back during the days when the United States and the Soviet Union were allies. The call, after passing through a battery of operators, finally reached its destination somewhere deep in the bowels of the Kremlin. As the connection was made, Roosevelt came on the wire and said, "Hello, Joe? It's Frank here. Giants three, Dodgers nothing."

By 1947 the baseball careers of pitcher George "Pinky" Woods and manager Jimmy Dykes were both on the downslide—Woods after pitching three years for the wartime Boston Red Sox and Dykes after playing twenty-two years and managing the Chicago White Sox for thirteen more. And so it was that the two of them found themselves in that great decompression chamber between the major leagues and oblivion known as the Pacific Coast League. More accurately, on the sixth-place entry in the Pacific Coast League, the Hollywood Stars. Dykes, who had been catching hell from the owner of the Stars, Bob Cobb, for not lifting his faltering pitchers soon enough, started Woods one afternoon. Woods walked the first four men he faced. Dykes slowly ambled out to the mound, hands thrust into pockets, to put into effect the boss's new edict. "Pinky," said Dykes, "the boss says I'm too slow changing pitchers. You're through." But, as Dykes reached for the ball, Woods offered up as an excuse, "Jimmy, I'm just barely missing the corners." Without missing a beat, Dykes grabbed the ball and replied, "You've just missed sixteen times and that's enough for me. You're through."

Back in 1947, just when you would have thought *The Sporting News* had exhausted its use of the word "phenom,"

the New York Giants brought up a young player named Clint
Hartung, who threatened to break the indoor record for the
number of times he inspired the use of the word. Hartung,
playing service ball in Hawaii during World War II, had pitched
and won twenty-five games without a loss, patrolled the
outfield in his spare time, and batted .567 with thirty home
runs in fifty-seven games. His bat held manna to scatter to
starved Giants' fans. Small wonder that writers covering the
Giants—a sorry club that had finished last in the National
League the year before and in the second division seven of
the previous eight years—looked upon Hartung as the team's
salvation, calling him "Superman" and "Baseball's Paul Bun-
yan" and, in tribute to his hometown, Hondo, Texas, "the
Hondo Hurricane."

It soon became woefully obvious, however, that Hartung
was something less than a sure bet for a direct pass to the
Hall of Fame, his glove and ability to connect with a curve
nothing to write home about. So, the same writers who at
the beginning of spring training had been writing about the
"Hurricane" now began to consider him something less than
a zephyr. One writer from the wire services, who had come
to discount the pious twaddle handed out by the Giants' P.R.
machine, viewed Hartung as nothing less than a wartime
accident, and expressed that sentiment in a syndicated story.
As luck would have it, the wire-service story "had legs" and
traveled much the same route as the Giants, appearing time
and again in many of the towns the Giants played in during
their final spring-training trip. Hartung had finally had
enough, not appreciating that it was the same story. Approaching the writer of the story, Hartung, with a look of
brooding malevolence, demanded, "Why do you keep writing
those terrible stories about me?"

Those sideshow guess-your-weight contests called pre-season predictions that every writer worth his typewriter feels compelled to offer his readers are often only a chance to show off the writer's unerring ability to be wrong. One such exhibit came before the 1941 season, when only one of the 262 members of the Baseball Writers of America correctly predicted that the Yankees would win the American League pennant and that the Dodgers, Cardinals, and Reds would finish in that order in the National League race. The writer was Charles Dexter of the New York *Daily Worker,* the party organ of the Communist Party.

World War II begot, ironically, more dimouts in the civilian sector and more night games in the baseball stadia. After baseball commissioner Kenesaw Mountain Landis decreed, "Wartime conditions of employment in Washington make it worthwhile to have more night games," the lights went on over D.C.'s Griffith Stadium. Others followed as the major leagues approved unlimited night ball despite the opposition of several of baseball's lords, including Branch Rickey, then the ruling mahatma of Brooklyn. Rickey, who prized a penny saved more than the next man—especially if it was his—stated his opposition in the plainest terms: "You don't have to pay for sunshine."

George "Catfish" Metkovich, one of the few wartime players to last past the Duration, came by his nickname honestly. Seems that prior to his tryout with the talent-starved Boston Braves in 1940, Metkovich had gone fishing. Landing a three-foot catfish, Metkovich put his foot on the fish's back while trying to extricate the hook. The catfish, somewhat less than pleased at its predicament, lashed out, and its sharp fin cut through the crepe sole of Metkovich's shoe. And through most of Metkovich's foot. The catfish's fin was ultimately removed in surgery—hence Metkovich's nickname.

Babe Ruth was more than just a name. He was an institution, worldwide. And so it came as no surprise that Japanese soldiers on the South Pacific island of New Britain accompanied their attacks on U.S. soldiers with shouts of "To hell with Babe Ruth!" believing it to be the ultimate insult to the American tradition. Ruth, informed of this slur on his name, reacted the way most Americans did during World War II: "I hope every Jap that mentions my name gets shot. . . . And to hell with all Japs anyway."

During his twenty-year career—a career that saw him pitch for more cities than Rand and McNally had on their maps—Louis Norman "Bobo" Newsom nonchalantly walked through life. And he always walked to his own drummer, calling everyone within hailing distance "Bobo," for example, and being called "Bobo" in return. By 1943 he found himself pulling his third tour of duty with the St. Louis Browns. His few good performances suspended like fruit in Jell-O, it seemed that Newsom was forever being relieved by Nelson

Potter. It got so that Newsom would approach Potter before a ball game and ask, "Say, Bobo, when are you and I pitching again?"

But Potter was not the only person coming after Newsom; ol' Bobo had neglected to pay some bills and was being sued by some of his creditors—always having been out to those he was into. Finally, after being knocked out of the box in his first seven starts, Newsom managed to finish a game. One of the local sportswriters, commenting on the improbable event, credited it to the fact that "He saw a sheriff in the stands and was afraid to leave the field."

By the end of the year Bobo had taken his act to Washington. For the fourth time. But even four times around didn't help Bobo with names. One afternoon, Washington sportswriter Bob Addie was sitting around the Shoreham Hotel lobby with fellow scribes Red and Lyall Smith, comedian Joe E. Brown, and his son and daughter-in-law, Mr. and Mrs. Joe E. Brown, Jr., when he saw Bobo approaching the group. Addie waved over ol' Bobo and, after receiving the obligatory "Hello, Bobo," from Newsom, made the introductions: "Bobo, this is Mr. Smith, Mr. Smith, Mr. Brown, Mr. Brown, and Mrs. Brown." Bobo, overwhelmed with all the names coming at him in a tidal wave, hesitated a moment and then said, "Well, if nobody is going to give their right name, then I ain't either," and walked away.

Long before George Steinbrenner was even a glint in his daddy's eye, Joe McCarthy was counseling his Yankees on the need to respect the Yankee pinstripes. And showing respect, according to "Marse Joe," involved wearing coats and ties. It seemed to work, for in sixteen years as manager of the Yankees, McCarthy won eight pennants and seven World Series titles, never finishing out of the first division.

Finally, in 1946, McCarthy packed it in. Two years later, however, he decided to return, this time as manager of the Boston Red Sox. One day a Boston sportswriter approached McCarthy on the potential for a clash with his star outfielder, Ted Williams, who never wore a tie, asking him what would happen if Williams ignored his coat-and-tie edict. McCarthy answered, "Any manager who can't get along with a .400 hitter ought to have his head examined."

Tommy Bridges plied his trade in the uniform of the Detroit Tigers for sixteen years, winning 194 games during the regular season and four more during World Series play. Bridges's fame was based primarily on his handiwork with the curve—at least, that's how the common thinking went. But there were those who thought that Bridges might just have been handier with the spitball. One of those was Paul Richards, his catcher.

Richards remembered the time Bridges was struggling to protect a one-run lead against the Washington Senators in the ninth inning with men on base and a pretty good country hitter by the name of Stan Spence at bat. Crouching down in his catcher's stance, Richards flashed a sign for a curve, but Bridges shook it off. Richards then gave the sign for the fast ball, and again Bridges shook him off. The change-of-pace? Nothing doing. Finally, running out of signs to deliver, Richards decided the only thing left was the spitter. It came down the pike, a real beauty. "Strike one!" bellowed plate umpire

Bill Summers. Now the battery mates went through the charade again. And again it came down to the spitter. "Strike two!" roared Summers as again Spence let it go, mesmerized by a honey of a pitch. This time around Richards didn't even bother with a sign. "What's the use?" he said to himself. He got ready and watched as it danced and back-filled its way to the plate: "Strike three!" Spence flung his bat away and screamed something at Summers that sounded like "spitter." Other Senators raced out to support Spence, all complaining about Bridges's use of an illegal pitch. Summers finally walked to the mound and addressed the supposed miscreant. "Tommy," he said, "there are some people who say you're throwing a spitter." Bridges put a look of hurt on his face, answering, "How can that be, Mr. Summers? The spitter's been outlawed for years. How in the world would I ever learn how to throw one?" And with that the defeated Summers retreated to his position behind the plate. Whereupon Bridges cupped his glove to his mouth and addressed Summers in a mock stage whisper, "Hey, Bill, wasn't that last one a doozy though?"

The only thing faster than Satchel Paige on the mound was Satchel Paige behind the wheel of a car. One time this hell-bent-for-leather driver drove his white Lincoln Continental through every stop sign in Los Angeles, whipped through safety zones so fast the people standing in them were an endangered specie, made U-turns without warning in the middle of busy thoroughfares, and generally tested the elasticity of the law. On the same barnstorming tour, Paige drove his Continental down a one-way street the wrong way.

Playing dodge 'em with his car, Satch ducked in and out, weaving his way around the oncoming cars. Finally a motorcycle policeman, siren blaring, pulled alongside Paige and hollered, "Pull over there!" Paige dutifully pulled over. The policeman dismounted and came over to Paige. As he neared the car, he asked, "Didn't you see the sign saying this was a one-way street?" Satchel looked up at the policeman with wide-eyed innocence and replied, "I was only going one way."

Tony Lazzeri's major league career wound down to a precious few games, just twenty-seven games in 1939, split between two teams. By the time he had taken his final at-bat for the New York Giants, Tony knew that his future lay elsewhere. And so, when the job as manager of the hapless Toronto Maple Leafs was offered, "Poosh 'Em Up Tony" jumped at the chance. The Maple Leafs, who had once had such glorious players as Nick Altrock, Ike Boone, Dan Brouthers, Bill Carrigan, Bill Dineen, Hugh Duffy, Bob Elliott, Buck Freeman, Charley Gehringer, George Gibson, Burleigh Grimes, Carl Hubbell, Wee Willie Keeler, Napoleon Lajoie, Heinie Manush, Frank McCormick, Urban Shocker, and Dixie Walker dotting their line-up, were now a tatterdemalion aggregation of once-wases and what-could-bes. In fact, the day Lazzeri inherited them, they had been held scoreless in thirty-odd innings.

Watching his hitless—and scoreless—wonders play, Lazzeri began to grow philosophical about his charges. And so when Walt Lanfranconi pitched a four-hitter for the Maple Leafs, giving up four scattered hits and no walks, and Toronto went down to a 2–0 defeat, the resigned Lazzeri approached his twenty-three-year-old right-hander and, throwing his arm around him in an avuncular manner, said, "Never mind, kid. Next time out you'll probably pitch a shutout. And with our slugging, you'll be sure to get a tie!"

Only the previous October Boston Red Sox shortstop Johnny Pesky had been the centerpiece of one of baseball's greatest moments. St. Louis Cardinal Enos Slaughter, his feet hollering "Gangway, here I come!" had barreled home while Pesky, momentarily distracted by the crowd noise and the movement of the base runner from first to second, had held the relay throw a nanosecond too long, allowing Slaughter to score the winning run in the seventh game of the World Series. Returning to his native Portland for the winter of 1946, Pesky tried to resume his life despite his recent notoriety. One of his pet diversions was attending all of the University of Oregon football games, where he was treated to the passing pyrotechnics of the Webfoot quarterback, Norm Van Brocklin. On the afternoon in question, the annual to-do between Oregon and Oregon State, neither Van Brocklin nor his opposite number had completed a pass in a carload; everything thrown in the vicinity of receivers was dropped. Finally, after yet another Van Brocklin pass had been dropped by an Oregon receiver, one of the fans in the stands behind Pesky, with a mixture of impatience and good humor, cried out, "Throw Pesky the ball . . . He'll hold on to it!"

Comedian Joe E. Lewis once cracked, "Show me a Philadelphia team and I'll show you a loser." And for years the

Phillies played as if they were out to prove Lewis right, finishing in or around last place almost every season. Their efforts were reflected in their attendance figures; the fans who came out to the little bandbox known as Baker Bowl wouldn't have crowded the head of a pin.

During one typical game—this one against the Cubs—with the score up in the paint cards and the fans, such as they were, up on their hind legs rooting for less, the denizens of the press box turned to pastimes other than baseball: namely, pelting each other with anything near at hand. First it was paper clips, then water cups, then water cups filled with water. As the merriment got out of hand and the water seeped between the press box's creaky floorboards, Phillies owner Gerry Nugent suddenly appeared in the doorway of the press box. "Gentlemen," he scolded the delinquents, "I'll have you know that we have fans sitting down there." That was enough for Chicago writer Warren Brown, who jumped to his feet and cried out, "God! What a story!"

Someone, we don't know who, once said, "If God hadn't invented J. G. Taylor Spink, then he should have." For almost a half-century, J. G. Taylor Spink was both *The Sporting News* and the game of baseball. The man whose name now adorns the award made every year by the Baseball Writers was the keeper of baseball's flame, giving full faith and credit to the game's murky traditions in the pages of his paper. He also looked upon himself as the keeper of his flock, calling writers from his offices in St. Louis at all hours—particularly the wee small ones of the morning.

And so it was one day that J. G., on his way over to

Brooklyn to cover a World Series game, hailed a cab in Manhattan driven by a citizen identified on his hack license as "Thomas Holmes, Brooklyn, New York." Spying the license, Spink asked the driver, "Are you Tommy Holmes, the baseball writer?" And then added, "The one who works for the *Brooklyn Eagle?*" The cabby responded, "I'm not, but some sonofabitch out in St. Louis thinks I am and keeps telephoning me at three in the morning. And, if I ever get my hands on that guy, I'll wring his damned fool neck. . . . " Spink, it was noted by those in the cab with him, was mum for the rest of the ride.

In the long history of baseball there have been two super-greats reputed to have the ability to read the signature on the ball on its way to the plate. The first was Rogers Hornsby, whose visual acuity was such that when he once let a borderline ball go by and the pitcher complained that it was a strike, the umpire retorted, "Mr. Hornsby will tell you when it is." The other was Ted Williams, whose "eye" was legendary. Once in Cleveland during a game whose significance was minus-ten on the Richter scale, plate umpire Hank Soar decided to test Williams's claim that he knew the strike zone better than any umpire. Soar deliberately called a strike on a pitch that was six inches outside. Williams said nothing at the time. But on the slugger's next time at bat he turned to Soar and said, "You know, that strike you called on me last time up was six inches outside." Caught, all Soar could answer was, "You're absolutely right!"

Joe Engel ran the Chattanooga Lookouts of the Southern Association with an iron hand from 1929 through the 1960s.

Some suggested, though, that the iron hand had been inserted into a velvet glove—a velvet glove that sometimes tickled. The man they called "the Barnum of the Bushes" once traded shortstop Johnny Jones to Charlotte in the Sally League for a twenty-five-pound turkey, and then invited some twenty-five sportswriters to a turkey dinner to taste the "new meat" on the team. After the dinner Engel claimed, "I think I got the worst of the deal. That was a mighty tough turkey." Another time Engel was engaged in a contract dispute with a young prospect. The youngster wired Engel: "Double my salary or count me out!" Engel promptly wired back: "1, 2, 3, 4, 5, 6, 7, 8, 9, 10!"

On the set of *The Pride of the Yankees,* in which Babe Ruth played himself, the talk had turned to the shirt-tearing scene in the Pullman celebrating a World Series victory. "The players didn't have to act that one," he said. "We ripped up one hundred twenty shirts—and at seven-fifty each." Then, in answer to the inevitable question as to whether it was *cinema verité,* Ruth answered, "Sure, we used to do that. I remember once Dutch Reuther came on the train with four shirts. We'd tear one off and he'd go back and don another. So we had to get 'the wrecking crew' again. He finally had to borrow a shirt to get off the train!" There were pajama-tearing celebrations as well, remembered Ruth, although these weren't included in the picture. "I remember once Colonel Ruppert wouldn't open his dressing room door for us, so we just broke it in and off came the pajamas. 'My, that Baby Ruth is a bad boy,' he said."

RAIN DELAYS

Legend has it that Early Wynn once told a reporter he knocked down his own mother, because, the story goes, his mom "was a helluva curve-ball hitter." But Early himself put the lie to the story. "It wasn't my mother I knocked down," he said. "It was my son. The kid had just lined a good curve against the fence. . . . The first rule of pitching is: the pitcher has to look out for himself."

The early 1930s were to cop a line, the worst of times for everybody in America. And baseball was no exception. One of those hardest hit was Philadelphia A's owner and manager Connie Mack, who, despite having had three consecutive pennant winners, was beginning to feel the pinch of the deepening Depression. His star-studded payroll had become a burdensom luxury in a day when most men, in the classic phrase of the day, couldn't even spare a dime. To raise capital Mack began dispersing his stars to the south, north, and west. All for cash on the barrelhead, of course. One of those sold was infielder Jimmy Dykes, who had put in fifteen years, including many on one of the most awful clubs in the history of baseball, the A's of the late teens and early '20s. Sent to the White Sox, along with outfielder Al Simmons, in 1932 for $100,000, Dykes returned to the A's in 1948 as a coach. Mack welcomed Jimmy back to the club at the winter meetings with a "Jimmy, I'm afraid we can't pay you enough money." To which the impish Dykes replied, "Keeeripes! Do we have to start in where we left off sixteen years ago?"

The
Fifties

In days of yore ballplayers oftimes trod the boards: Rube
Waddell appeared in a period melodrama called *The Stain of
Guilt;* Bill Hallman, a second baseman for fourteen years,
mostly with Philadelphia teams, was a regular on the old
Keith Circuit; "Turkey" Mike Donlin retired from baseball
after 12 years in the big leagues to play the Orpheum Circuit,
and on and on. But several ballplayers saved their acting for
the diamond. One of those was Pee Wee Reese, a player who
could play-act with the best. His Academy Award performances, so often unappreciated by others, were rewarding to
his teammates—in more ways than one.

Like the time the offerings of the Dodgers' starting
pitcher suddenly began to fall into the outfield more often

than into the glove of his catcher. Manager Charlie Dressen had had enough even if his pitcher hadn't, and signaled to the bullpen for Clyde King, his ace right-handed reliever.

King, however, required a long warm-up before he was effective, and so, while the reliever was delivering his practice tosses from the mound, Dressen instructed third baseman Billy Cox to run over to Reese and tell him to start up his "injured eye" routine. No sooner had Cox clued in Pee Wee than Reese began pawing at his eye, hopping up and down like Rumpelstiltskin in heat. And although they were thoroughly accustomed to Pee Wee's histrionics, the umpires were so moved by his Sarah Bernhardt-ing that they crowded around the "stricken" shortstop to see what aid and assistance they could render. With everyone crowded around the artful Dodger, Dressen was beaming, his ploy having given King the time to warm up to his maximum effectiveness. And then, all of a sudden, Reese felt the presence of another person, Clyde King himself, who put his arm around the "injured" infielder and pleaded, "Pee Wee, can I help, too?"

During the 1957 World Series a writer asked Milwaukee Braves pitcher Bob Buhl what he was going to do in the off season. "I'm going to Saginaw to help my father," Buhl replied to the writer. "And what does he do?" asked the writer, pen poised. "Nothing," replied Buhl.

On the eve of the opening game of the 1950 World Series between the Philadelphia Phillies and the New York Yankees, a silver-haired lady went from hotel to hotel in Philly in search of a room, but without success. Finally, she located a room across the river in Camden, New Jersey. "Are you a baseball fan?" politely asked the clerk, looking with a curious eye at the lady signing in. "Oh, yes, indeed," she answered. "My husband pitched the first ball in the 1924 World Series." With that the clerk looked down at the register and read, "Mrs. Calvin Coolidge, Northampton, Mass."

Billy Loes combined a fast ball and a devil-may-care attitude into a career that spanned eleven years and left many a manager shaking his head. Take the time he claimed he lost a ground ball "in the sun." Or the time he admitted to one and all that he didn't want to win twenty games, " 'cause they'd expect me to do it all the time." Or the time Brooklyn Dodger manager Charlie Dressen read that Loes had picked the Yankees to beat his team, the Dodgers, in seven games in the upcoming 1952 World Series. Dressen sought out Loes and demanded an explanation from his Dodger pitcher. Loes had one: "I was misquoted, Skip. I picked 'em in six!"

Sign stealing has been around as long as the game itself, a subtle form of larceny that has enabled teams to win games and even pennants. One of its great practitioners was Charlie Dressen, manager of the Brooklyn Dodgers during the early 1950s. Dressen, who put great faith in his resourcefulness—going so far as to tell his troops, "Stay close, I'll think of something," when they were behind—was so proud of his ability that when he addressed his team before the 1953 All-Star game, he told them, "Don't worry about the signals, men. I'll give each of you the signals used on your own team."

During the World Series of the same year, however, Dressen had the tables turned on him. New York Yankee Billy Martin, who had played under Dressen at Oakland—and was, as Pete Hammil once wrote, "The only Yankee to play like a Dodger"—noticed Dressen flashing the signal for squeeze bunt. Martin thereupon turned the stolen signal into a rally-killing out, thus assuring the Yankees of a victory over the Dodgers in the Series.

Don Larsen had just pitched the most memorable game in World Series history, a ninety-seven-pitch no-hit, no-man-reached-first perfect game. After the fifth game of the 1956 Series, as Larsen stood at his locker basking in the afterglow of his achievement and a noisy knot of newsmen gathered round, from somewhere out of the crowd came the voice of one writer long on *chutzpah* but short on intelligence. "Was this the best game you ever pitched?" the disembodied voice asked.

In 1950 Dom DiMaggio led the league in stolen bases with just fifteen, the lowest number of steals ever to lead a league. When DiMaggio showed up at a club meeting of the New York chapter of the BLOHARDS—an acronym for the "Benevolent and Loyal Order of the Honorable and Ancient Red

Sox Die-Hard Sufferers"—a loyal member moved over to the "Little Professor" on unsteady feet and asked him how he had come to lead the league with fifteen stolen bases. Dom could only smile and say, "Pesky missed the hit-and-run sign that many times."

Although no rule states explicitly that baseball must be played with just one ball, all the rules seem to point in that direction, referring to *"the* ball." But there was one occasion when two balls were in play, and it had to be determined which one was *the* ball. On June 30, 1959, in a game between the Chicago Cubs and the St. Louis Cardinals, Chicago pitcher Bob Anderson threw a pitch plateward to Stan Musial with the count 3–1. Home plate umpire Vic Delmore pronounced Anderson's delivery to be ball four. But Cub catcher Sammy Taylor protested, arguing that the ball had hit Musial's bat and should therefore be called a foul. While Taylor was arguing with Delmore, the ball skipped merrily on its way to the backstop, the umpire viewing the ball's flight as the direct result of having bounced off the catcher's glove.

While the contretemps was going on behind the plate, Musial, heeding the advice of teammates hollering "Run, run!" took off for second with the ball still in play—if Delmore's original call stood, that is. At that point Cub third baseman Alvin Dark came racing in, grabbed the wildly bouncing ball, and threw it in the direction of shortstop Ernie Banks, who was covering second. At about the same moment, Delmore absentmindedly handed Anderson another ball, which he also threw toward second. The Anderson ball sailed off into the wild blue yonder, and Musial, watching it disappear into center field, took off for third. But he had taken only a couple of steps when he was tagged by Banks, who had the ball from Dark, who had the ball thrown by Anderson for "ball four." Base umpire Bill Jackowski ruled Musial out because he had been tagged with the original ball, the ball in play. The Cardinals protested, but the call stood. As did Musial, completely puzzled by the presence of two balls in one game.

During the 1954 season Dusty Rhodes of the New York Giants had pinch-hit a total of forty-five times, delivering in the pinch fifteen times, often with home runs. The first time Rhodes had come to the plate as a pinch hitter for the right-handed Monte Irvin, Brooklyn catcher Roy Campanella had remarked, "Any club that's gotta pinch-hit for Irvin must be hurting." Rhodes showed just how much they were hurting by singling home the winning run.

Jump forward to the '54 World Series with Rhodes's Giants playing the Cleveland Indians. With the score tied at 2–2 in the first game, bottom of the ninth, the Giants were threatening with Willie Mays hugging second and Hank Thompson, intentionally walked to set up an inning-ending double play, perched on first. Giant manager Leo Durocher called the scheduled hitter, Irvin, back to the bench and instructed Rhodes to "get up there and hit one out." Rhodes, whose intention on entering the batter's box had been to take the first pitch, watched as Cleveland starter Bob Lemon hung a curve ball. That did it. Never one to keep an idea too long, Rhodes changed his mind and less swung at the ball than merely browsed at it with his bat. The ball hung lazily in the air and then descended, 257 feet, 8 inches from home, Plop! into the first row of the shortest left-field bleachers in the majors for a three-run homer, adjourning the proceedings *sine die*. As Rhodes rounded first, he chanced to look over at Lemon who stood agonizing as if he had been struck in the heart by an Indian arrow. Grimacing, he flung his glove high in the air. As Rhodes remembered it, "Lemon's glove went farther than the ball!"

There is absolutely no truth to the rumor that Dusty Rhodes thought a myth was a female moth. However, there is no hard-core evidence that he was a candidate for the Nobel Price in physics either. And so, when Rhodes, the hero of the 1954 World Series, was called upon to speak, anything could happen. One time Rhodes made a speech at the University of Alabama. After the speech, a professorial gentleman approached Rhodes and asked him where he went to college. Rhodes looked at the three-piece tweed jacket and said, "Professor, this is the first time I've ever set foot on a college campus in my life. As a matter of fact, I had a little trouble with grade school. Why," Dusty ambled on, "when I was promoted to the second grade I was so nervous I didn't dare shave for a couple of days."

By 1954 television had become a full-fledged medium, and it needed programs to fill its giant maw. One of the celebrities most in demand for personal appearances was the manager of the world champion New York Giants, Leo Durocher. On one occasion the Giant manager appeared on CBS-TV's "Name That Tune," a game show that required contestants to guess the name of a song for prizes. But when Durocher struck out on "Sympathy," host Bill Cullen offered some clues to help Durocher identify the song just played. "Leo," said Cullen, "suppose with the bases loaded the batter for the Giants hits what appears to be a sure triple and the umpire calls it a 'foul ball.' Fifty thousand fans are booing. Now, Leo, what does that ump need starting with the letter 'S'?" Without batting an eye, Durocher shot back, "A seein'-eye dog."

Even before Bo Jackson, there were two-sport athletes. The baseball-football quinella has included the likes of Ernie Nevers, Ace Parker, Steve Filipowicz, and 1950 Heisman Trophy winner Vic Janowicz. Janowicz played for the pathetic Pittsburgh Pirates in the early 1950s. He fit right in, batting .252 and .151 in his two years with the Pirates. Immediately after his second—and last—year in a Pittsburgh uniform, Janowicz signed to play football with the Washington Redskins. Against the New York Giants one Sunday afternoon in 1954, Janowicz made a particularly hard tackle that was heard all the way up in the press box. One press-box occupant, otherwise involved, looked up at the sound of the "thwack" and asked, "Who hit that ball carrier?" "Janowicz," came back the answer. The scribe thought a second and then said, "That's the first hit he's made all year."

The Pittsburgh Pirates of 1952 weren't the worst club in baseball history. But many would have put them in the competition and bet on them. One of those was manager Billy Meyer who, addressing his soon-to-be 42-and-112 team, started a team meeting with: "You clowns could go on *What's My Line* in full uniform and stump the panel."

Unable to convey anything that resembled baseball strategy to his sorry lot of athletes, Meyer tried a simple system of signals, but was never quite sure anyone ever got them. During one game the third-base coach flashed a signal for a steal. Nothing. Again he flashed the signal. Still no response. Finally, St. Louis Cardinal second baseman Red Schoendienst walked over to the reluctant runner and said, "When are you going to run? They've given you the signal three times and I'm tired of covering second base."

Waite Hoyt was known as "the Schoolboy," owing to his having been signed by the New York Giants right out of Brooklyn's Erasmus Hall High School. Hoyt proudly carried his Brooklyn origins—and accent—through twenty-one years in the majors and into a second career as an announcer for the Cincinnati Reds. And so it was fitting that one day at Ebbets Field, when Hoyt accidentally missed a step on his way up to the broadcast booth, one of the retainers at Ebbets Field ran into the press box seeking help and yelling, "Hert's Hoyt."

The New York Yankees of the late 1950s had more than their share of bousers and carousers of the first water. And scotch to boot. After wrapping up the 1958 American League pennant with more than a week left in the season, the Yankees began to lead the Night Owl League in bourbon quarries visited, bed checks missed, and nocturnal mishaps. Word leaked back to Yankee general manager George Weiss that the Yankees had more hangovers than the gardens of Babylon, and he determined to put an end to such florid libels against nature far after the normal bewitching hour. And so he hired a private detective straight out of central casting— Panama hat, brown-and-white shoes, garish yellow sports jacket, the whole nine yards. In short, the P.I. stood out like the proverbial hand digit.

On duty, the P.I. stood around the lobby of Detroit's Statler Hotel, hoping to blend in with the furniture and pass himself off as a fan. Trying mightily to engage one of the Yankees in conversation after a night game, he finally singled out Whitey Ford, the Yankee left-hander. "Excuse me," he ventured, "but I'm a big fan from up in the Peninsula and don't get down to the games too much. I don't recognize any of the players. Which ones are Ford and Mantle?"

Ford, who had been tipped off by some of his teammates, spotted Bobby Richardson and Tony Kubek, the Yankees' candidates for the Clean Livers Hall of Fame, just going out the door for some late-night refreshment. "Ford and Mantle?" Whitey said. "There they go now!" "Thanks!" said the operative, racing off in the direction of the departing twosome and almost running into the revolving door. The next morning Ford encountered the counterfeit duo and asked, "Where'd you guys go last night? You seemed to be in one helluva hurry." "We were," replied Richardson. "There's a place that makes great sodas and they don't stay open past twelve-thirty, so we wanted to make it in time."

The Fifties

For fifty-one long years, baseball teams kept their headquarters and hindquarters in the cities where God and Kenesaw Mountain Landis intended them to be. The first hints of wanderlust came in 1953, as the Boston Braves dropped hints that they were Milwaukee-bound. Spring training continued apace, however, even though plans were afoot to move the team lock, stock, and franchise to Wisconsin. And so it was that, as the Braves played an exhibition game against the Dodgers in Vero Beach one early March day, two sets of sportswriters surfaced to cover the Boston-cum-Milwaukee Braves—those from Boston wearing caps with "Bs" on them and those from Milwaukee wearing caps bearing the letter "M." One of those from Boston who refused to believe that Boston was destined to become a one-team town pointed to his hat and remarked, "We're the Boston Braves. That other thing, the 'M'," he said, pointing, "stands for Maybe."

Baseball attendance figures became big news in the 1950s, a natural extension of the interest in big business during boom times. And one of the favorite arguments among those newsmen who followed them and filed them was whether to use the "paid" figures or the "overall" figures in stories. During one of those interminable arguments that always seem to take place in the press box during a lull in the game, an advocate of using the paid number argued eloquently, "If they dropped an atomic bomb on the joint would it get everyone or just those who had bought tickets?"

As a manager Frankie Frisch was a walking volcano in flannels. Especially when the team he was managing was the woebegone Chicago Cubs, a group that resembled a ball club only in the fact that they had gloves—even if they didn't use them. Such was their ineptitude that their double-play combination was known among the faithful as "Miksis-to-Smalley-to-Addison-Avenue." One day in 1951 Frisch, still fuming over what he considered an early ejection the night before, handed in the line-up card with an "I hope we get a better game than the one you gave us last night" growl. Plate umpire Bill Stewart, he of the New England accent and the rabbit ears, heard the growl and, answering the thought rather than the words, turned on Frisch, yelling "Y'routa the game" and flashed him the big motion, thumb extended.

Before departing from the scene, Frisch abused the mother tongue as best he could and then turned on his heel and strode in the direction of the dugout. As Stewart turned his attention to the field, he heard a commotion off in the direction of the Cub dugout. Suddenly something came hurtling out of the dugout, landing not far from Stewart. Stewart bent over to pick up the object, a book, and as he turned it over he could read the title, *Quiet Street,* a gift from the banished Frisch.

Rogers Hornsby may have been one of the greatest players in the history of baseball, but he fell far short of that standard as a manager. By the time he came to the helm of the Cincinnati Reds in the 1950s, Hornsby had had five tours of duty as a manager—and been fired five times. But rather than adapt, Hornsby maintained his hard attitude toward his players. As manager of the Reds he wouldn't even bother going out to the mound to take a pitcher out; he'd simply climb to the top step of the dugout and beckon to the poor unfortunate with one finger, leaving the embarrassed pitcher to walk the last mile unescorted. Nor was that enough punishment, for Hornsby would plop the pitcher down beside him on the bench to watch the rest of the game and never utter a word to him.

One afternoon one of his shell-shocked pitchers was showering alongside his bulldog of a manager when he happened to glance down and see Hornsby nonchalantly eliminating on his, the pitcher's, leg. Rather than maintain a polite fiction, the pitcher, now both pissed off and pissed on, hurriedly got out of the shower, dressed, and made straightaway to general manager Gabe Paul's office to register a complaint. "Mr. Paul," said the unfortunate, "y'gotta stop him." "Stop who?" asked Paul, contemplating his team's poor play and equally poor gate receipts rather than paying strict attention. "You gotta stop Hornsby. He was just pissing on me in the shower." Paul finally got the gist of the message, but could only turn around to his charge and say, "What would you like me to do?"

Baseball superscout Ed Libertore tells of the time Billy Martin took his Yankee teammates Whitey Ford and Mickey Mantle on an off-season hunting trip. Or at least that's what it was supposed to be. But what it really was was a practical joke that backfired. Literally.

The hunt was on a farm owned by a friend of Billy's who had told Billy beforehand he had a horse that had to be done away with. And that Billy would be doing his friend a favor if he would mercifully dispose of the hobbled horse. Without telling his two companions it was a put-up job, Martin took aim at the unfortunate horse and fulfilled his part of the bargain. But what to his wondering ear should occur but a second report from behind him. Turning around, Billy saw Mantle, his face irradiated with a dim, religious light, standing over a second fallen horse, his gun barrel still smoking. "I got mine!" Mickey yelled to Martin—who had to make good to his friend the price of the second unfortunate horse.

They tell the story of the little old lady who, in the 1950s, came up to one of the members of the Beat Generation and asked, "Does the crosstown bus go down this street?" To which the bearded poet laureate of the Lower East Side replied, snapping his fingers, "Do-dah, do-dah." Getting across town was not any easier for members of the Brooklyn Dodgers, who had to drive through the Battery Tunnel and up the West Side Drive to travel from the friendly confines of the Gowanus over to the Polo Grounds to meet their crosstown rivals, the New York Giants.

One night, Pee Wee Reese was at the wheel and three of his Dodger teammates—Duke Snider, Rube Walker, and Carl Erskine—were riding shotgun, when a cop pulled the car over just as it came out of the tunnel. As the cop parked his bike and walked back to the car, Snider said, "Okay, Pee Wee, show us your stuff." Reese handed the cop his Kentucky license, which read "Harold H. Reese." The cop said, "Where do you work, Mr. Reese?" no sign of recognition behind his shades. Reese, ever the gentleperson, said, "I'm employed by the Brooklyn Dodgers." The cop said, "The Dodgers! Hey, you're not Pee Wee Reese, areya?" Pee Wee answered in the affirmative and then did the gentlemanly thing, introducing each of the other occupants of the car. As a clincher, he added, "We're on our way to play the Giants tonight and I guess we were pushing it too hard." The cop said, "Listen, Pee Wee, I love you guys. Good luck tonight and I'm sorry I bothered you." Pee Wee downshifted and smiled at Snider. "Was that good enough, Duke?" he said, laughing.

The next night was Snider's turn to drive. Same route and almost identical scene as Snider put his foot to pedal and roared up the West Side Drive. Again, a motorcycle cop pulled the car over, but this time a different cop. Watching the cop dismount, Reese said, "Okay, big boy, now let's see you do your stuff." Snider pushed his wallet through the window, showing his license, which read "Edwin Donald Snider," and then went into his song and dance. "I'm Duke Snider of the Dodgers, and these are my teammates, Reese, Walker, and Erskine. We're on our way to the Polo Grounds for tonight's game."

The cop looked at the license, then back at Duke, and said, "I don't like baseball." With that, Snider got red in the face and said, "I don't like cops, either, so just give me the damned ticket!"

Hoyt Wilhelm rode one pitch, his knuckleball, straight into the Hall of Fame. For twenty-one years, the rubber-armed right-hander worked wonders with that one pitch, a butterfly with hiccups, that dipped and doodled and befuddled batters and catchers alike. In fact, when Wilhelm broke in as a twenty-eight-year-old rookie in 1952, he challenged any of his New York Giant teammates to catch three out of five of his knucklers. None, including Willie Mays, came close. The pitch was such that one manager, Billy Rigney of the Minnesota Twins, once confessed, "I hate to see my guys bat against him. They swing three times before the knuckler is halfway to the plate."

If Cal Abrams were to be remembered for anything, it would be for making his run home a marathon route in the deciding game of the 1950 season, his legs declining to fulfill the obligations they had sworn to, and being thrown out at home to end a Dodger rally, thus allowing the Phillies to win the game—and the pennant—in the next inning. He might also be remembered as one of the lesser novas on a team filled to the Plimsoll mark with such superstars as Jackie Robinson, Gil Hodges, Roy Campanella, Carl Furillo, Duke Snider—and just about anybody else you could select. And that becomes the crux of the story. Back when the Dodgers—and Brooklyn—were in full bloom, the Dodgers were more than just Brooklyn's civic pride, they were its being. And that was reflected in its hero worship of its players. Adding to that hero worship was Happy Felton, who had a Knothole Gang made up of youngsters from the greater New York area who would appear on his radio show after home games to compete for prizes on the field and interview players. Felton had a standing offer to any member of the Dodgers: $50 if they appeared on his post-game show as a judge to select the best of the three performing little leaguers and an additional $50 if the winning little leaguer selected that player to be interviewed in the dugout at the end of the show. Well, all season the winning little leaguer had been selecting the likes of Robinson, Hodges, Campanella, Furillo, Snider, et al. And all season long, Robinson, Hodges, Campanella, Furillo, Snider, et al, had been picked by Happy Felton's producer to be the Dodger who would pick the best little leaguer. That was $50 and $100 a show if the same Dodger was selected by the winning little leaguer to be interviewed. While $100 might not be much to some of the Dodgers, making big salaries in those pre-inflation days, it was a substantial amount to Abrams, then getting the $6,000 minimum wage. And so every day Abrams would approach the producer to ask him when it was going to be "my shot" to be on the show. And every day, the producer would tell him he would get to him. Come the next to last day of the season, and the producer finally told Abrams that this was "his shot." Abrams, trying to maximize the opportunity, pulled aside one of the three little leaguers and told him that whatever he did that day, "You're the winner . . . tell him I'm the one you want to interview." Agreed. And so, after hitting the ball to all three little leaguers, Abrams solemnly declared that the little leaguer he had the pre-arranged deal with was "the winner." Now, Happy Felton turned to the winning little leaguer and asked, "And who do you want to talk to?" And from the mouth of a baseball babe came the answer, "Carl Furillo."

Danny Murtaugh was a no-bullspit sort of man who managed the Pittsburgh Pirates not once but four different times. His square chin and bulldog face belied his almost rocking-chair attitude. He rarely lost his temper, but once, subjected to a variety of shouted maldictions from one of the Pirates' faithful one day, he turned on the heckler—but with a disarming charm that was vintage Murtaugh. Approaching the fan—who was the sort you would use if you were developing a blueprint for an idiot—Murtaugh asked sweetly, "May I tell you something?" "Sure," answered the fan, more than somewhat taken aback. "When I was a youngster," Murtaugh went on, "I lived on a farm. We had a jackass on the place that just wouldn't do anything. Well, one day I gave that jackass a beating and my father heard the jackass hollering and came to his rescue. Then he gave me the beating of my life for what I had done and gave me some advice. 'Son,' he said, 'someday that jackass is going to haunt you.' And you know," said Murtaugh, turning away and finishing his parable over his shoulder, "I never believed him till now!"

The record books are full of attendance figures for the most this or the most that, but they rarely publicize the lowest number of fans attending a game. If those numbers cannot be located in any record book, however, they abound in baseball lore. There is the story, for example, about the Pirates game in the 1890s attended by six paying customers, and another about the time threatening weather and intermittent showers reduced the "crowd" at a Pacific Coast League game to exactly one paying patron. Whereupon the plate umpire took the megaphone and addressed the stands thusly: "Dear sir, the batteries for today's game are. . . ." More recent lore is full of tales about the St. Louis Browns, the team Bill Veeck purchased in 1951. Moving John Lardner to write, "Many critics were surprised to know that the Browns could be bought; because they didn't know the Browns were owned." And if many didn't know the Browns were owned, many more didn't even know they existed. So when Veeck received a phone call from a fan, who asked "When does the game start?" Veeck answered, "What time can you get here?"

Bill Veeck inherited the culls and dredges of baseball when he took over the St. Louis Browns in 1951. One of those he found on his hands was Henry Irven "Bow Wow" Arft, a pedestrian left-handed first baseman then hitting in the .250 range and going downhill with a rapidity that would put him in the running for an Olympic Gold at Lake Placid. Trying desperately to unload his merchandise and at the same time pick up some hard-to-find funds to cover his expenses, Veeck wired his good friend and former partner, Hank Greenberg, now the general manager at Cleveland. Unfortunately, Veeck's telegram jammed and printed the message as "ARF-ARFARFARFARF." The same day Veeck received a telegram from Greenberg: "I CAN'T STOP LAUGHING. KEEP THAT DOG IN ST. LOUIS."

On Sunday, August 19, 1951, baseball's premier promoter and professional gadfly, Bill Veeck, believing that all promotional gimmicks were transferable ("You just change the gag line"), resurrected an old James Thurber short story about a midget who played baseball and inserted his own into the St.

Louis Browns line-up in the person of three-foot seven-inch Eddie Gaedel. Wearing elf's shoes, the number ⅛ on his back, and carrying a bat that looked like a conductor's baton, little Gaedel took his place—or, at least, part of a place—in the batter's box. As home-plate umpire Ed Hurley challenged Browns manager Zack Taylor on the propriety of sending a midget to the plate—not that it mattered to the Browns, then on their way to another hundred-loss season—Detroit Tiger catcher Bob Swift went out to the mound to visit with pitcher Bob Cain. Trying to keep a straight face, Swift imparted what little wisdom he could: "Keep it low." Nevertheless, Gaedel walked on four pitches that couldn't have found his mini-strike zone with a Geiger counter.

Ralph Kiner had reason to feel pleased with himself—he had just led the National League in home runs for the seventh consecutive year. And so, during the winter of 1952, he went home to San Diego secure in his knowledge that his efforts would be rewarded by the Pittsburgh Pirates even though the team as a whole had hardly done as well—finishing with a miserable 42–112 record, a full twenty-two-and-a-half games out of seventh. When his contract came in with a $5,000 cut in salary, Kiner could only think that it was some sort of mistake. Never having bothered to send his contract back, Kiner reported to the Pirates training camp the following spring and went in to see general manager Branch Rickey. As Rickey sat behind the walnut garbage chest he called his desk, dropping ashes from his cigar like a volcano all over his shirt front and bow tie, Kiner made his misgivings about the contract known and suggested to Rickey that it must have been a mistake. Rickey heard him out and then, punctuating the air with his cigar, replied, "Young man, we could have finished last without you. . . ." Case closed.

The outlook wasn't bright for Chicago White Sox manager Jack Onslow that spring training season of 1950. The previous year, Onslow's first at the Sox's helm, his team had limped home sixth, thirty-four games behind the pennant-winning Yankees. If players were dominoes, the 1949 White Sox would have been a collection of double zeros. Now Onslow sought to get his team, if not within hollering distance of the top, at least within hailing distance of the first division. But even with off-season trades that brought Chicago the likes of Nellie Fox, Hank Majeski, and Phil Masi, and promising rookies in the wings like Chico Carrasquel, Onslow knew that the White Sox still possessed a compilation of disorders that would take more than a few good men to cure. In short, the White Sox suffered from a morale problem. And so, he decided that something, anything, had to be done to shake his team up.

One of the plans he hit upon was to bar wives from spring training camp. Politely he asked his players to refrain from bringing their brides with them. All complied. All, that is, save one outfielder, who brought his wife to camp. The wife, an aggressive, obnoxious woman, attended every exhibition game played by the Sox, offering her comments, gratuitously, on the progress of the team. Onslow tried his best to get her to quit camp, or at least quiet down, but to no avail. "I'm here and you can't put me out," she bellowed. "Where my husband goes, I go too," she added. Finally

Onslow had had enough. "Madame," he shouted back, "how would Beaumont suit you?" And that's where he shipped the outfielder, bag and baggage, the next day.

With the possible exception of the time a midget took it upon herself to sit on J. P. Morgan's lap at a congressional hearing, nothing that has occurred in the hallowed halls of Congress could rival the appearance of Charles Dillon Stengel—who went by the name of "Casey"—in front of the Subcommittee on Antitrust and Monopoly in July of 1958. The subcommittee, then investigating baseball's possible exemption to the antitrust laws, had invited the Yankee manager and one of his players, Mickey Mantle, to testify on the laws then being considered. Casey, who rambled on for a couple of hours on God-knows-what, pausing occasionally to sort out a mixed case or find a dropped reference, finally allowed his autopilot to slow down long enough to mutter, "They talk of the slow pitch and the fast ball, but what about Phil Rizzuto who has all those daughters?"

After listening to Stengel's syntax for another hour or so—a strangled style of address known as "Stengelese"—the subcommittee chairman, Estes Kefauver, turned to Stengel's co-witness, Mickey Mantle, and asked him if he "had any observations with reference to the applicability of the antitrust laws to baseball." Mantle came up to the microphone, shuffled his feet, adjusted his hands to just the right fold, and said, "My views are just about the same as Casey's."

The tieless and tireless Bill Veeck first burst upon the baseball scene with the Cleveland Indians in 1946, and in three short and exciting years broke all attendance records, won the World Series, and moved on. Veeck surfaced again in 1951, this time with the St. Louis Browns, baseball's poor relation.

Scrounging around for a way to make money, any money, Veeck hit upon the idea of petitioning his fellow club owners for a share of their radio and TV revenue. His reasoning went something like this: it takes two teams to make a game, and his Browns contributed in that way, even in the losing. Some of the owners, such as Connie Mack and Clark Griffith in Philadelphia and Washington, respectively, gave him a sympathetic audience and acceded where their local rights amounted to mere pennies. But New York was something else entirely. There the rights were worth big bucks. And the man who had the say-so over the sharing of those big bucks was Yankee general manager George Weiss, who would tear the skin off a flea if it meant money. Weiss heard out Veeck and his proposal and then turned on Veeck and demanded, "When you were doing more than two million in attendance in Cleveland, why didn't you offer to split your radio with everyone else? Why all of a sudden now?" The unflappable Veeck merely replied, "Circumstances alter cases."

It was a moment as indelibly etched on the baseball land-scape as the faces on Mount Rushmore, the moment when Bobby Thomson hit "the shot heard round the world" and won the 1951 pennant for the come-from-behind Giants over the Dodgers in a three-game play-off. After the game the joyous Giants entered their clubhouse to a deafening silence;

all the newsmen were congregated on the Dodgers' side awaiting the triumphant return of the team that had gone into the ninth three runs to the good. But they soon remedied their mistake and began to seep into the Giants' locker room, first in a trickle and then in a Niagara of writers, photographers, and radio men. It finally got so the players could hardly move. Through it all, Thomson noticed one small man struggling harder than the rest of the sea of invaders to get closer. Finally he got close enough to shout, "Bobby, we want you to appear tonight on the *Perry Como Show* and we'll give you five hundred dollars." Thomson said he was sorry, but he wanted to spend the evening with his family and that, anyway, the Series against the Yankees started the next day. The little man, still struggling like a salmon against the current, wouldn't take no for an answer and hollered back, "We can give you a thousand." Suddenly Thomson's Scottish ancestry got the better of him and he hollered back, "For a thousand my family can take care of themselves for an evening."

The St. Louis Browns of the late 1940s would do anything to win. Anything! They even hired a psychologist who doubled in hypnosis, Dr. David F. Tracy. Trying to get the Browns out of their mental underwear, he took a team that had finished dead seventh in 1949, with 53 wins and 101 losses, and in 1950 spurred them to finish with 58 wins and 96 losses, still mired in seventh.

It was during the 1950 season a young pitcher came to him complaining of a sore arm. Tracy put the pitcher under hypnosis, making him raise his arm well above his head and lower it slowly. He told his charge that when he awoke the arm would be as "good as new," and that all the pain would be gone. He then roused the sleeping beauty with one snap of the fingers. "How does that right arm feel now?" inquired the good doctor. "Great!" the pitcher replied. "Trouble is, I'm a lefty."

Yogi Berra has become as famous for his language as for his performance on the job. Berra once decribed a restaurant in Cleveland as "so crowded no one goes there any more." When Joe DiMaggio asked him, "What time is it?" he answered, "You mean right now?" When he received a "Day," he thanked "everyone who made this day necessary." Asked what he'd do if he found a million dollars, he said, "If the fella who lost it was poor, I'd return it."

But perhaps the line that started the Berra legend for one-liners came when manager Casey Stengel tried to take his green catcher in hand and break him of his habit of swinging at bad balls. "Study the pitcher carefully," cautioned Casey. Berra listened attentively and then proceeded to swing at three balls that were not even on nodding terms with the strike zone. Upon returning to the bench, and to Stengel's withering stare, Berra threw down his bat and growled, "Whaddaya expect me to do? Swing and think at the same time?"

Dizzy Dean and the Queen's English were never at one. In fact, when somebody once asked Dean if he "knew the

Queen's English," he replied, "Of course, I do. And I also know the King's English too."

After completing his colorful big-league career, Dean turned to broadcasting and began trampling everything within earshot, Queen's and King's property alike. "He slud into third" was the first of his many well-publicized departures. Later he varied "slud" with "slood." Another time he used the word "ain't," and when anti-semantic fans bombarded the station with complaints about his grammar, he first said, "Sin tax? What won't they think of next?" and then added, "Many people who don't say 'ain't' ain't working." But the one Deanism that befuddled supporters and detractors alike was the one, "The trouble with them boys is they ain't got enough spart." Pressed for an explanation, Dean said, "Spart is pretty much the same as fight or pep or gumption. Like in the 'Spart of St. Louis,' that plane Lindbergh flowed to Europe in."

The MacMillan *Baseball Encyclopedia* is one of the most comprehensive tomes ever put out, rivaling for number of entries the Manhattan telephone book—with very few numbers left unlisted. Leaving not stone unturned, no gravestone unexamined, the committee of researchers strives for accuracy. Despite typographical errors—Wade Boggs is listed as a left-handed throwing, right-handed batting third baseman—it comes as close to perfection as any baseball book ever has.

Every now and then, however, a glitch pops up. Such is the case with an entry that read "Lou Proctor, B. Unknown." Mr. Proctor, according to the *Baseball Encyclopedia,* played one game for the St. Louis Browns in 1912, and is credited with a walk in that game. But Lou Proctor was actually a press-box telegraph operator who inserted his name into a box score one day to become something everyone wants to be: a major league player.

Thirty-nine years later, it took Eddie Gaedel another 39 years to get into the encyclopedia as a St. Louis Brown with his entry of one walk. Unlike Proctor, Gaedel actually went to the plate to do so—all three feet seven inches of him, which is more than Lou Proctor's (non) statistics show him to be. All of which prompted St. Louis sportswriter Bob Broeg to start his post-game interview with Gaedel by saying, "You're what I've always wanted to be, and ex-major leaguer."

Ever since Father Moses first came down from the mount with his heavenly interview engraved on two tablets, reporters have viewed it as their sacred duty to soak up the local color, literally—visiting all the local water holes and consuming all of the products of Scotland, save perhaps the rye bread. One sportswriter who firmly believed that the deficiencies of the day could be made up the following night in the company of Thomas and Jeremiah was Arch Murray, who covered the New York Giants for the New York *Post* during the '40s and '50s. Murray, a champion tippler, would often show up somewhat the worse for wear in the middle of the game, his eyes looking like road maps, and invoke the help of whatever unfortunate he sat next to, copying his neighbor's box score doodlings.

One day, in the middle of a Giants–Cincinnati Reds game, Murray ambled into the press box somewhere in the middle of the game. All the other working nonstiffs tried desperately to take up two seats so that there would be no room for the Murray-come-lately. Murray finally located an unoccupied chair down at the end of the press box and fell into it. Muttering something that sounded like "Catch me up," Murray took out his unsullied scorebook and began to make the appropriate marks in the appropriate boxes as his neighbor replayed the game, droning on "Westrum fouled out, Stanky out short to first," etc., etc. All these trivialities Murray heard, much as a tired man hears a tune in the railway wheels.

Finally, the helpful reporter came to the notation beside Lockman, "FO 9," and, investing it with some feeling, said, "Lockman hits a helluva drive to right, but Post makes a great catch." Murray, who had been lounging in his seat, suddenly pulled himself up proud and said, "I'll be the judge of that!"

Home runs are a thing of beauty and a joy forever. Hank Greenberg, when asked if he had any superstitions, replied, "Yeah, when I hit a home run I remember to touch every base." Another favorite home run story is told by Garry Maddox, who, when asked to describe his major league grand slam, thought for a minute and then said, "As I remember it, the bases were loaded. . . ."

Al Rosen remembers one of his 192 lifetime four-baggers. Seems that Rosen had just blasted one into the Municipal Stadium left-field stands and, after doffing his hat, came down the steps into the Cleveland dugout. But there was nobody there to greet him. They were all around Luke

Easter, who had fallen asleep on the bench and been awakened by the crowd's roar in response to Rosen's homer. "He jumped to his feet and bumped his head on the top of the dugout," recalled Rosen. "Knocked himself out cold."

The Wrigleys were to Chicago what the Windsors are to England: the leading family. And, not incidentally, the most vulnerable to press criticism. When William Wrigley was criticized by a Chicago writer who wrote under the name "Bill Bailey," he cornered the writer, better known as Bill Veeck, and told him, "If you think you can do a better job, then you're the president." And for the next fifteen years, Veeck ran the Cubs. Wrigley's son, Phil Wrigley, was also sensitive to criticism published in the Chicago papers. And so when the Chicago *Daily News* sports editor ran a story and accompanying box in the paper soliciting Cub fans to vote for a new manager, Wrigley had to be restrained from running a Cub-sponsored ad asking readers to choose a new sports editor for the paper. Ironically, when the Wrigley family sold the Cubs, they sold it to a newspaper.

Ever wonder what those on-the-field conversations are about? Johnny Evers, of Tinker-Evers-Chance fame, who won the nickname "Crab" not only for his sidling moves toward a ball but for his overall demeanor, would often jump up and down in front of an umpire, waving his arms in the air, all the while asking the official how his family was, or when they were going to have dinner together, or some such social nicety that belied his movements. The fans in the stands, seeing the Crab go through his act, would cheer him on, sure that he was giving the ump a hiding.

Another who would go through on-the-field charades was Cleveland Indians manager Lou Boudreau. Umpire Frank Umont remembers Boudreau coming out of the dugout, ostensibly to argue a call. Arriving in front of Umont, Boudreau started jumping up and down, but his words were something like, "Frank, how in the hell can I manage a team where the clean-up hitter's batting only one forty-eight?"

But perhaps the most unusual on-the-field conversation came when New York Yankee pitcher Eddie Lopat, pitching a tight 0–0 game into the eighth inning, put the two leadoff men on base and began to feel his stomach churning. Unable to fight the jitters, Lopat called his catcher, Yogi Berra, out to the mound. While the overflow crowd at Yankee Stadium could only assume that Lopat had called Berra out to discuss what pitch to throw slugger Gus Zernial, who was flexing his rather sizable muscles in the batter's box, Lopat greeted Yogi with a "Know what the penalty is for bigamy?" The astounded Berra could only mutter, "Dunno." Lopat, already feeling more at ease, responded, "Two mothers-in-law." Yogi could only shake his head and trot back to his place behind the plate. And Lopat, now totally relaxed, proceeded to strike out the tough Zernial.

The Sixties

Right after the Cincinnati Reds had beaten the Giants in a game in 1968, a young sportswriter wandered into the Reds' locker room. The lost writer was looking for winning pitcher Gerry Arrigo, but, lacking that sixth sense that the fourth estate prides itself on, had mistakenly singled out second baseman Tommy Helms. "Nice pitching, Gerry," the writer-hyphen-lost-puppy said to Helms. Helms, picking up on the misplaced patter, shot back, "Nothing to it." That opened it up, or so the reporter thought. Now, with pencil poised he prodded his subject: "You didn't seem to have any trouble with Mays or McCovey." "They're nothing," said Helms, warming to the task. "I throw McCovey a few curve balls and he's dead." The reporter's eyes widened as he began scribbling furiously. "And Mays is even easier," Helms went on. "I can beat the Giants any day in the week. I just throw my glove on the mound and they're dead." Unfortunately for the callow reporter, soon to be in need of employment, the story found its way into print. And when it did, Reds manager Dave Bristol duly noted it. The next time a reporter asked Bristol if Arrigo would pitch against the Giants, he looked the reporter in the eye and replied, "Hell, no! I'm gonna pitch Helms."

Whitey Ford tells a story about the 1961 All-Star Game held in San Francisco. Six Yankees were selected to the American League squad, Ford and Mickey Mantle among them. When Ford and Mantle, the inseparable dynamic duo, arrived in the city, Giant owner Horace Stoneham, the host of the game, told the two that they could go to his country club if they wanted to play some golf. The two decided to take Stoneham up on the offer. And that's not all they took, charging everything they could think of to Stoneham's account—sweaters, balls, greens fees, everything. Without bothering to inform Stoneham, they ran up about $200 on his tab.

That night Stoneham was at the traditional All-Star party always held the eve of the game, along with some of the players, including Ford and Mantle. Ford remembers approaching Stoneham, who had "a sly smile on his face. I offer him two hundred dollars, but he won't take it. Instead, he says, 'Let's make it double or nothing. If Willie Mays gets a hit off you in the game, I win, and you and Mickey owe me four hundred dollars. If not, we're even.' "

Ford, caught with his hand in the cup, had little choice but to agree. The next day Ford was the starting pitcher for the American League. In the first inning he retired the first two batters. The third, Roberto Clemente, doubled, bringing Mays to the plate. Ford got two quick strikes on Mays and then decided to load up on a spitball. As Ford tells it, "The pitch breaks from above the shoulders to his knees. Strike three. Out in center field, Mickey is going crazy, running in hard, clapping, whooping. I could just imagine those announcers in the TV booth solemnly pronouncing to fifty million people what a great competitor Mickey is: 'Look how much he cares in the first inning of the All-Star Game.' "

Frank Lucchesi, who would ultimately go on to manage in the majors, was serving his time as manager of the Pocatello, Idaho, minor league club in the 1960s. Lucchesi's managerial genius approached that of a man who could rewrap a new shirt and not have any pins left over. One day, with his team at bat and the score 2–2 in the bottom of the ninth, his lead-off batter singled up the middle. Now Lucchesi wanted a bunt to move the base runner into scoring position. The set of signals called for the next thing Lucchesi touched after his hat to be the sign for the batter—his pants for the bunt, his ear for the steal, etc.

As Lucchesi touched his hat, he felt a kamikaze mosquito buzzing his ear. Without thinking, Lucchesi slapped at the mosquito and then dropped his hand to his trousers. Too late. The base runner at first was already off and running, heading for second, having interpreted Lucchesi's slap at the mosquito as the steal sign. The opposing catcher promptly reared up and threw the ball into center field. With the base runner heading for third, the center fielder, in turn, picked up the ball and threw it past the third baseman, allowing the base runner to score the winning run.

After the game Lucchesi was approached by a writer who asked, "I heard you're a daring manager. That was the time to call for the bunt, wasn't it?" Lucchesi knew that the mosquito had won the game for him, but instead of telling it like it was, he misled the reporter, telling him, "Yeah, but you got to play dangerously. We practiced that one in our morning workout."

The mosquito? Lucchesi missed him, too.

Baseball and baseball writers have been an item since Henry Chadwick first put pencil to papyrus to chronicle many of the very first organized games. Throughout the years those who have toiled as pencil-pushers have included a few Pulitzer Prize winners and many more who would have qualified for the P. U.-litzer Prize, with the majority somewhere in between.

Back in the early 1960s, one group of young writers took it upon themselves to enliven the game through their reporting. And their questioning of players. Jimmy Cannon likened their continual nattering to that of chipmunks, and that became their unofficial title. They included Larry Merchant, Phil Pepe, and Stan Isaacs, among others. But it was Isaacs who gave them their proudest moment when, after the final game of the 1962 World Series, a group of reporters cornered winning pitcher Ralph Terry in the Yankee locker room. In the middle of the interview, Terry was called to the telephone to talk to his wife, who had given birth a few weeks before. Returning to the horde, Terry was asked, "Who was it?" "My wife," Terry responded. "What was she doing?" another asked. "Feeding the baby," answered Terry. "Breast or bottle?" asked Isaacs.

It was Yogi Berra who said, "It ain't over 'til it's over," but it was Donn Clendenon who knew from first-hand knowledge what Yogi was talking about, even if Yogi didn't. Clendenon, playing for the Pittsburgh Pirates, was facing the great Warren Spahn in a game that was heralded as Spahn's final appearance in Pittsburgh. In one inning Willie Stargell was scheduled to be the first batter up, followed by Clendenon and Bill Mazeroski. Just before the Pirates went to bat, Maz approached both Stargell and Clendenon and said that they ought to all strike out for Spahn. "It's going to be his last game here and it would be good for the fans," Maz told his two teammates. So they all agreed, and all struck out. And the fans rewarded Spahn with a big hand.

But it wasn't to be Spahn's last year, for the next year, 1965, he came back as a pitcher and pitching coach for the New York Mets—leaving behind him one of baseball's best bon mots: "I'm probably the only guy who worked for Stengel before and after he was a genius." And Clendenon? He was livid. "That made me mad," said Clendenon. "I strike out enough on my own when I'm not trying to strike out and I had to give one away to a guy who didn't quit."

Cakes are a recurring theme in baseball. Many's the ballplayer who has taken off his flannels and sat down on his bare haunches atop a cake sent to the clubhouse by their groupies. And then there's the cake that Casey Stengel presented to the prototypical early Met, Marv Throneberry, but didn't quite pass it over to him, because, as Stengel said, he "was afraid he'd drop it."

Casey himself was the beneficiary of a cake on the occasion of his seventy-fourth birthday in 1965. The night before, the enormous cake—four feet wide, three feet high, weighing over 600 pounds—was wheeled into Shea Stadium to be presented to the manager of the Mets. The baker, asked why it was presented to Casey the night before his birthday and not on his natal day, said, "It wouldn't stand no more." "Why didn't you just put it in a cake box?" asked Stengel.

It was a widely held belief that Milwaukee Braves pitcher Lew Burdette possessed a wet one, a spitter, something baseball looked down on as an illegal pitch. One who looked down, literally and figuratively, on Burdette's favorite pitch was Dodger first baseman Norm Larker, who, during an at-bat against Burdette's offerings, complained to plate umpire Frank Secory that Burdette was throwing spitters. Secory, however, disagreed. "Those pitches were sinkers," he said. "Oh, yeah," challenged Larker. "Well, one of them 'sinkers' just splashed me in my right eye."

Charlie Finley was a notorious nickel nurser, so parsimonious, it was rumored, that anyone who dropped a buffalo head near him would lose a knuckle trying to redeem it. One of the stories that went the rounds to prove that the man threw nickels around like manhole covers had to do with Finley and Joe DiMaggio. After DiMaggio was hired as vice president of the Oakland A's, he asked Finley for a desk. Finley reportedly replied, "I'm not here all the time so you can use mine. Here, this drawer is yours!"

Ron Davis, picked up in a midseason trade in 1968 by the St. Louis Cardinals as pennant insurance, was asked by one reporter how it felt to go from the last-place Houston Astros to the first-place Cards. Just as Davis cranked up his answer, fellow outfielder Curt Flood broke in, "Oh, he's been all right since he got over the bends. They put him in a decompression chamber right away."

After Baltimore's Jim Palmer threw a no-hitter at the Oakland A's back in 1969, one writer was heard to say: "Well, there goes the A's 113-game hitting streak."

Jim Ray Hart, an infielder who played for the San Francisco Giants for parts of eleven years during the 1960s and early '70s, was hit by pitches so often that his teammates nicknamed him "Mr. Dent." One of the Giants explained Hart's style thusly: "Hart always has a toothpick in his teeth when he goes to bat. If he thinks the pitch is going to break the toothpick, he pulls his head back. He doesn't like to get his toothpicks broken."

Ghostwriters go back as far as Cyrano de Bergerac. They've been part of the baseball landscape ever since somebody "authored" Abner Doubleday's supposed invention of the national pastime. Over the years, those who have served as literary impersonators for famous ballplayers have included Ford Frick, Bozeman Bulger, Warren Brown, Bill Corum, Joe Williams, John Kieran, H. G. Salsinger, Ed Danforth, Sid Mercer, Hype Igoe, J. Roy Stockton, Gene Fowler, and Damon Runyon, to name but a few. The fact that they often penned their "ghosted" articles for athletes who hadn't the foggiest of what was being submitted under their bylined names was attested to as early as 1924, when the editor of a Washington paper complained, "I wanted to give Babe Ruth a nice boost during the [Washington Senators–New York Giants] Series but couldn't find him." He had tried in vain to locate Ruth through a certain writer who was "cooperating" with Ruth and filing the Series reports under Ruth's name. "You write the Babe's stuff, don't you?," he asked the writer. The ghost, without a conscience, laughed it off, replying, "Why, I haven't talked to the big stiff for over two weeks."

In recent years the ghost–player tandem has produced enough books to stock a new wing of the Library of Congress. One of those was Willie Mays's biography, *My Life In and Out of Baseball*, written "with" San Francisco sportswriter Charles Einstein. Over the course of the 1965 season Einstein sat down with Mays and made notes of his reminiscences of the game and his career. When the season ended, Einstein collected all of the notes and sat down at his typewriter. Unalbe to understand a few of his scrawls, he called Mays for clarification. "Hello, Willie, this is Charley," Einstein started in. A long silence ensued from the other end of the phone. Finally, Mays said, "Charley who?" "Charley Einstein," came the answer. Again there was a long silence, although Einstein could hear breathing. A little desperate, Einstein added, "You know, Charley Einstein, the fellow who is doing the book with you." Again a pause, and then, "What book?"

When Bobby Bragan took over the reigns of the Milwaukee Braves from Birdie Tebbetts in 1963, the new manager chanced to find two envelopes in his desk drawer marked "No. 1" and "No. 2." Alongside the two envelopes was the cryptic message: "Open in emergency only." As the season progressed and the Braves didn't, Bragan found himself in the same clubhouse looking at the same desk. It was then that he opened the envelope from Tebbetts marked "No. 1." The message read: "Blame it on me." The next year was little better, with the Braves moving up, almost imperceptibly, from sixth to fifth. Bragan was in need of comfort and sought it in "No. 2." Opening the second envelope, he read the following: "Prepare two letters."

Expansion ball came to the majors in 1961, and with it came the long and short of baseball. For the new Los Angeles

Angels had drafted behemoths Steve Bilko, weighing in at 250 pounds, and Ted Kluszewski at 245, and on the other end of the scale, they had also drafted two men who would never hear the words "jump ball," little Albie Pearson, at five foot five and 140 the smallest man in the majors, and Rocky Bridges, five eight and 170 pounds, soaking wet. As fate, and the traveling secretary, would have it, the two men who resembled Macy's Thanksgiving Day floats were put into one room and the two men the size of hot walkers into another across the hall. Bridges, who could find humor in an accident—as he did once when he woke up from a beaning and asked, "Will I be able to play the violin?" and was assured that he would, which drew the response, "Funny, I never could before"—called the traveling secretary and suggested that the room assignments be switched. "Otherwise," said Bridges, "the hotel will tilt."

How do ballplayers know it's over when it's really over? In 1949 Buddy Blattner, a sometime second baseman for the Philadelphia Phillies, had what he described as a "season-long slump." The next year he did something about it, retiring and going into the broadcast booth. Another sometime player who, like Blattner, went into broadcasting when his playing days were over was Bob Ueker. "Uek," who had more pink slips than a well-dressed lady, remembered how he knew it was over: "They broke it to me gently. The manager came up to me before the game and said they didn't allow visitors in the clubhouse."

One of baseball's great unwritten rules is that the bat should always be held with the label, or trademark, up so that, in baseball parlance, you can "read it." Once, when Hank Aaron came to bat against the Los Angeles Dodgers, catcher John Roseboro looked up and saw that Hank had rotated his bat so that the trademark was facing out. Roseboro cautioned Aaron, "Hank, your bat is facing the wrong way!" Aaron scornfully looked down at the Dodger catcher and uttered one of baseball's most oft-repeated classics: "I didn't come up here to read. Came up here to hit!"

Fred Hutchinson was the kind of manager who wouldn't just throw chairs, he'd throw entire rooms. Never one to mince words, he would "tell it like it is," even before the phrase gained popularity in the mouth of a TV cartoon posing as an announcer. On one occasion, as manager of the 1962 Cincinnati Reds, "Hutch" watched pitcher Moe Drabowsky load the bases on walks. "All of a sudden," remembered Drabowsky, "I went to three-O and with every pitch, I heard a strange noise from the dugout: Hmphfff!" After one more pitch, and one more "Hmphff!" the Hmphfff-or charged out to the mound to talk to his pitcher. "Moe, look around you, what do you see?" said Hutchinson. "The bases are loaded now. You've got no place to put this guy. Get the sonuvabitch out!" And with that he went back to the dugout. Fortunately, Drabowsky did!

Eddie Sawyer, who managed the 1950 edition of the Philadelphia Phillies—"Whiz Kids" and all—to the National League pennant, was brought back by the owners to run the

Phillies a second time around. But after finishing seventh in 1958 and eighth in 1959 and watching his sorry group of athletes lose the first game of the 1960 season, the forty-nine-year-old Sawyer retired, this time for good. His explanation: "I want to live to be fifty."

At the 1962 New York Baseball Writers Dinner, one writer, playing the role of Los Angeles Angels's general manager Fred Haney, Bill-Baileyed the following takeoff:

> Won't you come home, Belinsky?
> Won't you come home?
> You've chased around all night.
> You'll be tomorrow's pitcher,
> You need some rest,
> You can't win if you're tight.
> 'Member that great no-hitter
> That brought you fame?
> You spoiled it for some floozy dame.
> A star you could be,
> If you'd stick to tea;
> Belinsky, won't you please come home?

The Belinsky in question was Robert, better known by his nickname, "Bo," and for being a carouser of the highest—or lowest—order. During his brief sojourn with the Angels, Belinsky won almost instant fame for pitching a no-hitter for the expansion club and for squiring around some of the most eligible females in the Hollywood community, including—but hardly limited to—Joan Collins and Mamie Van Doren. One night during spring training the year following his arrival on the baseball scene, Belinsky and Van Doren were an invitem at every night spot in the Palm Springs vicinity. As the bewitching hour of twelve neared—the hour that Angels's manager Bill Rigney had mandated for curfew—Bo was still tripping the light fantastic with Mamie. "I'm sorry, I gotta go or I'll miss bed check," offered the apologetic Belinsky, quite out of character. "I know, honey," cooed Mamie, "I'm dancing as fast as I can."

When Casey Stengel, the manager of the newly minted New York Mets, was asked why his team had made catcher Hobie Landrith its number-one choice in the 1961 expansion draft, he answered, " 'Cause if you don't have a catcher you'll have all those passed balls."

Casey Stengel was never one to use one word where a hundred would do. Especially when he had a point to make. One afternoon the press crowded around the manager of the newborn New York Mets to ask him about his prospects. Stengel looked around and pointed at two of them, youngsters Ed Kranepool and Greg Goosen. "See that one there," he said, pointing at Kranepool. "In ten years he has a chance to be a star." And then Stengel pointed in the direction of Goosen and said, "In ten years the other guy has a chance to be thirty."

The 1962 New York Mets were truly, as manager Casey Stengel called them, "Amazin'." They managed to lose 120 games, more than any team in modern history. And most of them in ways theretofore unknown to humankind. One of those times came when Mets antihero Marvelous Marv Throneberry ripped a long drive into the outer reaches of the Polo Grounds' greensward and came roaring into third ahead of the throw. But lo and behold, there was the umpire holding his hand in the air and proclaiming Throneberry out for not touching second. As Stengel came charging out of the dugout as fast as his aging legs could carry him to do battle with the umpire over the injustice, third base coach Cookie Lavagetto intercepted him. "Forget it, Case," he whispered, "he didn't touch first either."

Wes Westrum inherited the pitiable New York Mets in 1965 from Casey Stengel and found them in their natural resting place: last. The next year the scenery changed ever so imperceptibly, with the Metsies rising above their level to ninth. But 1967 found them on their way to another last-place finish and hundred-loss season. Westrum, trying something, anything, to rouse them from their torpor, called a team meeting of the club out in Los Angeles. Addressing the concert assembled, Westrum admonished them, "Okay, from now on, no more broads in the hotel rooms." From the back of the room pitcher Jack Hamilton yelled, "You mean it was okay before this? Nobody told me."

The expansion Houston Colt .45s were on the cusp of breaking a record as old as baseball itself: losing an entire season's series to an opposing team. Many teams had lost every game but one to an opponent—the 1927 Browns to the Yankees, the 1937 Reds to the Pirates, the 1945 Reds to the Cubs, and the 1909 Braves, to both the Cubs *and* the Pirates—but no team had ever lost every game played against a single club. Now the 1962 Colt .45s were well on their way into the record books for negative accomplishments, having lost the first fifteen out of the eighteen scheduled games to the Philadelphia Phillies. With the final three-game series opening in Houston, the Colt .45 management scheduled a "Break the Jinx" night, but to no avail—the Phillies swept a double-header, running the streak to seventeen with but one more game to play.

Before the next night's game, Houston somehow came up with a witch doctor—or at least someone dressed up in a witch doctor's costume—who gave a voodoo dance in front of, on top of, and around the Phillies' dugout. With the witch doctor doing that voodoo two Phillies from Latin American countries, Tony Gonzales and Tony Taylor, refused to come out of the clubhouse until he was removed from the scene. He was, but apparently not before his black magic had worked its wonders. The Colt .45s—suckers for a rite—won that night and avoided a new record for futility.

When Stan Musial retired after the 1963 season he took with him half of the National League records and almost all of the St. Louis Cardinal team records. Five years later, to commemorate Musial and his contributions, the Cardinals dedicated a massive ten-foot bronze statue on a marble pedestal in front of Busch Stadium to honor "the Man." At the ceremonies, Cardinal manager Red Schoendienst, who had been Musial's teammate for fifteen years, was called upon to say a few words. Schoendienst looked at his former teammate and then, addressing the crowd, said, "Stan, in your twenty-two years as a player for the St. Louis Cardinals, you've done a lot for them . . . and for baseball. Now you're going to be doing something for the pigeons."

After his playing days—pedestrian by any standard—were over, Joe Garagiola became an after-dinner speaker of Hall of Fame proportions. On one occasion, he spoke at a banquet along with the governor of Arkansas, Orville Faubus. After studying Garagiola's name in the program, Faubus stood up and said, "In the hills where I come from we would take a name like that, get two girls' names out of it, and have enough left over for three boys."

Jimmy Piersall was one of baseball's most colorful characters. Most prolific as well, sharing the all-time major league record for most kids with Paul "Dizzy" Trout, each of whom sired ten. After much practice, Piersall managed to reduce the fundamentals of diapering his offspring down to basic baseballese: "First, you place the diaper in the position of a baseball diamond, with you at bat. Next, fold second base over home plate. Place the baby on the pitcher's mound. Then pin first base and third base to home plate." It worked!

The Sixties

After agreeing to appear on a radio talk show with sports broadcaster Jack Buck, Yogi Berra was handed a check for twenty-five dollars made out to "Bearer." Berra studied the check for a second and then said to Buck, "Jack how long have you known me? How the hell could you spell my name like that?"

Dick Stuart was called, for good reason, "Dr. Strange-glove," "Stonefingers," and other less-than-complimentary nicknames during his career as a first baseman who looked as if he were carrying his glove for a friend. When Stuart got married, he introduced his new bride to a sportswriter with a prideful, "You know, behind every successful man there stands a good woman." The sportswriter blinked and could only respond, "With a first baseman's mitt?" Stuart's inadequacies were such that once, when the public-address announcer intoned that anyone interfering with a ball in play would be ejected from the field, Pirate manager Danny Murtaugh was heard to remark, "I hope Stuart doesn't think that means him."

When Floyd Caves Herman, better known as just plain ol' "Babe," joined the Daffiness Boys of Brooklyn back in 1926, it was a perfect fusion of souls with both teammates and fans. For even though Herman was what Rogers Hornsby called "the perfect free swinger"—he averaged .340 for his six years in a Brooklyn uniform and holds both the highest batting average ever for a Dodger, .393 in 1930, and the all-time Dodger record for slugging percentage, .557—Babe Herman's deficiencies in the field and on the base paths left his account sorely in the red. How else to explain the fact that *twice* in one year he was passed on the base paths by a base runner who had hit a homer; or that he once doubled into a double play, winding up at third with two other equally misdirected teammates? Still, his bat served long after his playing career had wound down—a career that saw him batting .346 at the age of forty-one in the Pacific Coast League and then coming back to the wartime Dodgers for a thirty-seven game finale which he began in typical Herman fashion, singling in his very first at bat and promptly tripping over first base.

When he stopped playing for good, Babe began a career as a major league superscout. Many's the time other scouts sought Herman's advice on a prospect—his opinion of the phenom's chances was $99^{44}/_{100}$ percent infallible. He was also reputed to be the best "closer" in the scouting fraternity—which gives us the makings of a story, a story that took place back in the spring of 1948.

It seems that that year there was a world-beater out of Meridian, Idaho, named Vernon Law and every scout west of the Mississippi, Herman included, was beating a path to the youngster's door. Forming something like a parade into the living room of Law's mother, the scouts regaled her with the wonders of having her son pitch for their team. Finally, it was Herman's turn to make his pitch for the club he represented, the godawful Pittsburgh Pirates, who in the previous two years had compiled the worst record in all of baseball. Herman began his spiel, extolling the virtues of the Pirate organization, an organization, he assured Mrs. Law, that "would look after her son . . . from the chairman of the board, Mr. Galbraith, to the executive vice president, Bing Crosby, down to . . ." But before Herman could continue with his rehearsed speech, Mrs. Law, a curiously intense expression on her face, asked, "Do you mean Bing Crosby, the singer?" Herman, sensitive to a chance to sign a prospect, quickly discovered that Crosby was Mrs. Law's favorite performer and assured her that if she would wait until that night to make her decision, he would have Bing Crosby personally call her.

Hurrying back to his motel Herman got through to the Pirate front office and told them of his plight—and potential. Could they find Crosby and have him call Mrs. Law at six o'clock that evening? He then hied back to court Law, arriving shortly before six to await the promised phone call. Sure enough, at six the phone rang. Mrs. Law picked it up and with an expression that was somewhat stronger than astonishment heard the voice announce that he was Bing Crosby. But even as she stood there listening, she couldn't quite believe it was he. And so, to satisfy her skepticism, she asked the voice to sing her favorite, "White Christmas."

And with that Vern Law became a Pittsburgh Pirate, winning a total of 162 games for the Pirates, including two in their 1960 World Series win over the Yankees. And every year thereafter, Bing Crosby would call Mrs. Law on Christmas to sing another rendition of his famous "White Christmas," all courtesy of Babe Herman, superscout.

Paul Foytack was a long-ball specialist for the Los Angeles Angels in 1963. The only trouble was, Foytack didn't hit long balls, he gave them up. Pitching against the Cleveland Indians in the sixth inning of a game on July 31, Foytack threw a pitch that Woody Held smashed for a home run. Indians pitcher Pedro Ramos, he of the lifetime .164 average, was up next. Bang, into the seats. Next, Tito Francona came—no, make that *rushed*—up to the plate. He, too, teed off on a Foytack delivery and sent it downtown for the third straight home run. The next batter was rookie infielder Larry Brown, a good glove man but mediocre hitter. When Brown sent another Foytack delivery into the stands—for his first major league home run—Angels manager Bill Rigney hurried to the mound to ask Foytack to sample the Lifebuoy in the showers. Foytack, whose giving up four straight homers in a row was a record, was later to tell reporters, "I was trying to knock Brown down with that pitch, so you can imagine what kind of control I had."

It was one of those interminable games, with little or nothing happening down on the field below. And so, as happens from time to time, the arrested adolescents upstairs in the press box had begun to string together names of all-time teams—the all-food team: Pie Traynor, Cookie Lavagetto, Bob Veale, etc.; the all-city team: Claudell Washington, Daryl Boston, Dallas Green, etc.,; the all-animal team: Bob Moose, Ted Lyons, "Goose" Goslin, etc.; and on and on ad nauseum. Finally, the talk turned to an all-prison team and the name Gates Brown came up. And with it the story of Joe Falls, the Detroit sportswriter who had walked up to Brown, the one-time convict then playing for the Tigers, to ask him why he wore the number 26 on his uniform. "Because they wouldn't give me my favorite number," answered

Brown. "What's your favorite number?" asked Falls. "The one I wore as a kid," said Brown. "What was that?" "Number 5081782."

After losing both his fast ball and his job with the Yankees, Jim Bouton wanted to stay on in the majors in the worst way. And that's what he did, finding himself on the pitching staff of the expansion Seattle Pilots. Bouton, who had pioneered the kiss-and-tell sports biography, was able to add several chapters to his book about his experiences with the Pilots. Once he explained that the toughest job any ballplayer had was explaining to his wife why *she* needed a penicillin shot for *his* gallbladder infection. But the quintessential Bouton story came when, returning home after one long road trip, Bouton hollered out to all the ballplayers being greeted by their wives: "Look horny, guys!"

It was one of those typical every-man-to-his-battle-station brawls that comes only after a beaning, with the *tout ensemble* of both teams teeming onto the field, more to stay out of trouble than to get into it. As the players of the Expos and the Pirates began pairing off, six-foot-six, 250-pound Montreal reliever Dick Radatz singled out little five-foot-five, 145-pound Freddie Patek of the Pirates as his quarry. With no sinister intentions in mind, Radatz put his arm around Patek, almost engulfing him in the process, and said, "I'll choose you and a player to be named later."

RAIN DELAYS

Ted Williams came back in 1969 to manage that "team" in name only known as the Washington Senators. What he found was a team that couldn't hit; it couldn't field or play either. After the Senators had lost an early-season game in which their hitting, pitching, and fielding were something less than professional, Williams called a team meeting. Locking the door behind him, Williams strode to the front of the locker room. After a long silence, the manager, struggling to control his emotions, turned to address his woebegone athletes. "Gentlemen," he began, "that was the worst exhibition of baseball it has ever been my displeasure to witness. I'm afraid we're going to have to start at the very beginning." Then, reaching for a ball from a nearby box, he held it aloft and, his voice dripping with sarcasm, said, "Now this, gentlemen, is a baseball." From somewhere in the back of the hushed room a hand shot up in the air. It was the mammoth hand of Frank Howard, the Senators' massive six-foot-seven slugger. "Uh, Skip," said Howard, "would you mind taking that a little slower?" Williams dissolved in laughter, breaking the tension.

Many's the ballplayer who comes from a place where a fellow has to walk around a dog enjoying a nap on the sidewalk. One of those was catcher Ed Bailey, who hailed from the small burg of Strawberry Plains, Tennessee. Before the 1962 World Series, some of his teammates on the San Francisco Giants were riding him before a game at Yankee Stadium. "Ed," asked one of the Giant catchers, "would you say there are more people in this park than there are in Strawberry Plains?" Bailey looked around the cavernous stadium slowly and then, as if he had figured it out with the accuracy of a census taker, said, "You know, there are more people in the bullpens here at Yankee Stadium than there are in Strawberry Plains."

Red Smith, the fabled sportswriter, was covering one of his many World Series. And all the other sights that went with it, including the local watering holes where he traditionally ordered his favorite lubricant, "without fruit." The merry men known as the Baseball Writers had scheduled an early-morning tour of the host city's more famous historical spots, and Red, in one of his less lucid moments, had signed up to accompany them. Only trouble was, the tour started at nine in the morning, scant hours after Red had ended his previous night's tour.

About a half-hour before the scheduled start, one of Red's colleagues decided to call up his room to rouse him. And to get a rise from him. Enlisting the help of one of the junior men on the writers' block, they composed a message that went something like this: "Mr. Walter Smith? This is the Casino Pool Hall. You were in last night and forgot your cap. Would you like to pick it up or would you prefer we deliver it?" Well, after about twenty rings the receiver was lifted and a disembodied voice grunted "Hello!" Immediately, the junior writer, sure of his quarry, began to read his prepared speech. There was a silence on the other end of the phone, and then Smith spoke up. "Would you look inside the cap? And if there's a head there, would you be so kind as to send it over right away?"

The life of a relief pitcher ain't all it's cracked up to be. More times than not the rent a pitcher pays for his space on the pitching staff as a reliever is boredom. In days of old, he was given the added responsibility of being keeper of the "valuable bag," the bag of baubles, bangles, and beads that the rest of the team deemed worthy of safekeeping during the game. But once he was relieved of those responsibilities, the reliever had to make do and create diversions. Or be bored spitless. Many's the reliever who has engaged one of the charming "groupies" hanging out near the bullpen in conversation or called the concessionaire over for a hot dog or two. Other non-busybodies have read books, played cards or word games, or even gone to sleep in the bullpen.

It remained for Kansas City Royal reliever Dan Quisenberry to come up with a new alternative to twiddling his fingers. Stuck out in the farthest recesses of Cleveland's Municipal Stadium, Quisenberry was trying mightily to concentrate on what had, by then, turned into a Royal romp. With little else to do, he made friends with the spiders building their webs around the unused bullpen. Figuring he would be on more than a nodding acquaintance with them for a long time, he even gave them names, calling them in turn, Herman, Louie, Wally, and Gertrude.

Perhaps the most creative way to spell relief from boredom occurred to Moe Drabowsky, a reliever who plied his trade for seventeen years for more cities than Rand-McNally has on their road maps. Drabowsky, ever a blythe spirit, figured out the phone number of the opposing team's bullpen and, imitating the opposing manager's voice, would call up and order his opposite numbers to begin warming

The Sixties

up—at the strangest times, say when their team was ahead
12–0 or so. Drabowsky used his ploy sparingly, so it took a
long time for opposing managers to figure out why their
relief corps always seemed to be up and throwing.

The Seventies

One of the craftiest pitchers ever to take the mound was right-hander Don Sutton, who in his twenty-plus years of pitching amassed over 300 wins. As well as several complaints that he was "doctoring" the baseball. But finding evidence that Sutton was actually tampering with the ball was not easy. One time an umpire, convinced that Sutton was applying a foreign substance to the ball, strode out to the mound to inspect Sutton's glove. What he found was a note: "You're getting warm, but it's not here."

Charlie Finley had just conducted a thorough house-cleaning, selling the remnants of his great Oakland team like items at a garage sale. Here a Joe Rudi to Boston, there a Vida Blue to the Yankees, and everywhere another member of the A's. When Sal Bando was asked how it felt to become an ex-A, he replied, "How did it feel to leave the *Titanic?*" But baseball commissioner Bowie Kuhn nixed the wholesale sales, citing some rule "for the good of baseball," and the players reverted to their old clubs. Yankee manager Billy Martin, somewhat miffed that the commissioner had voided Blue's becoming a member of the blue pinstripes, alluded to a swap the previous year between two Yankee pitchers— which they called "a life swap, not a wife swap." Martin said, "If Kuhn can nullify that, he's gotta talk Petersen into giving Kekich his wife back."

During his years as manager of the Boston Red Sox, Don Zimmer was known as "the Chipmunk." And for good reason, his jaw always distended by the constant presence of a chaw of chewing tobacco wedged firmly in his cheek. One day a call went against the BoSox and Boston first baseman George Scott, who rarely lost his temper, lost his and began arguing with umpire John Shulock. Zimmer took up the call and raced across the diamond to take Scott's place, preserving the negotiability of his star in the line-up while also contesting the call of Shulock. During the course of the ensuing argument, Zimmer took his chaw out of his cheek and slammed it to the ground. Shulock, who also chewed, retaliated in kind, slamming his chaw down. Next Zimmer went to his pouch of tobacco in his back pocket and slammed it to the ground; and again Shulock mirrored Zimmer's move, throwing his pouch to the ground. But then, the next thing anyone saw was

Zimmer on his hands and knees. Seems that when he had slammed his chaw down, his dental plate had stuck to the chaw, and Zimmer had to get down on his hands and knees to get his teeth out of the chaw he had thrown.

Cleon Jones proved he had been hit on the foot by a ball in the 1969 Series by showing plate umpire Al DiMuro a shoe-polish mark on the ball. Three years later, Jim Kremmel of the Texas Rangers loosed a pitch that went all the way to the backstop, and Chicago White Sox batter Eddie Leon protested to plate umpire Larry Barnett that the same thing had happened to him, pointing out the black smudge on the ball. Barnett gave Leon first base—even though the White Sox that year wore white sox and *red* shoes.

Stand-offs and stare-downs on the mound between a pitcher and one of his teammates trying to talk to him are fairly common. But one of the most unusual episodes in this never-ending type of confrontation occurred back in 1974, when St. Louis third baseman Joe Torre came running in toward the mound, which was occupied at that moment by Cardinal reliever Al Hrabosky. As Torre approached the man they called, with good reason, "the Mad Hungarian," Hrabosky's famed "controlled rage" got the better of him and he screamed out, "Wait a minute," stopping Torre in midstride. "If you want to stand on the mound, you'll have to ask me first. It's *my* mound!"

The term "absent-minded" has often been applied to professors and the like, but rarely to a baseball manager. But then again, managers like Johnny Lipon are far less common than professorial types. When Lipon managed the 1971 Cleveland Indians—serving out his sentence as an interim replacement for the fired Alvin Dark with the worst team in all of baseball—he gave new meaning to the phrase. Seems that Lipon, who had a habit of constantly fidgeting and moving things around in his hands, had just waved relief pitcher Steve Mingori into a game. When the left-hander arrived on the mound to meet with Lipon, the manager, who was holding a line-up card in one hand and the ball in the other, gave his pitcher the usual "Go get 'em!" line. Having delivered the little exhortation, he gave Mingori the line-up card and headed toward the dugout clutching the ball.

The World Series is at once the most prestigious and the most pretentious event on the American landscape. Most prestigious because no other event has captured the head-lines or the imagination of the American public so intensely or for so long a period. Most pretentious because it bills itself as a competition for the baseball championship of the world, when it is, in reality, only for the championship of a quadrant of the Western Hemisphere. But when New York Yankee owner George Steinbrenner was challenged on the parochialism of the event after the 1978 Series, he replied, "Well, we beat everybody who showed up!"

Hank Aaron was as efficient at answering questions as he was at hitting the ball. Especially during those trying times when, approaching Ruth's Everest of 714, reporters dogged his every step with questions. One writer, for whom baseball was only a passing fancy, tried a fancy pass with, "What do you look for when you hit?" Aaron, realizing the man's credentials were peccable, answered, "The baseball."

After fourteen-and-a-half years as a pitcher of ordinary proportions on the field—although he did make the Baseball Trivia Hall of Fame by being the last American League pitcher to steal a base before the designated hitter rule went into effect—Terry Forster finally gained a measure of fame because of his rather ample physical proportions. After watching an Atlanta Braves baseball game, "Late Night" host David Letterman called Forster "a tub of goo . . . the fattest man in all of professional sports." But Forster refused to be ruffled by his sudden notoriety, saying only, "When I looked in the mirror I thought, 'You know, he's right.' "

Forster later appeared on Letterman's show to dish it out with the TV personality. Toting three bags of M&Ms, a Nestlé's Crunch, seven hot dogs, a David Letterman sandwich from a nearby delicatessen (three slices of bread, pastrami, salami, cole slaw, and "lots of tongue"), and several other condiments all designed to make him thick to his stomach, Forster dished it out as well as packed it in with his host. The final clincher in Forster's repertoire of belly laughs was his one-liner, "You know, the waist is a terrible thing to mind!" But although Forster claimed as his ambition to lower his ERA, the man most likely to exceed never even lowered his ERA to match his weight—a hefty 250.

When the New York Mets acquired Willie Mays in 1972 for a player and $50,000, he was but a flickering image of what he once had been. The gilt of his greatness having peeled off for all to see, his receding skills allowed only occasional bursts of the light that had made him glow but a few short years before. But even if this national monument had become more than slightly tarnished, he still was a monument for the millions of New Yorkers who remembered him fondly for his exploits as the "Say Hey Kid" for the New York Giants before their move west. Now Mays was a gate attraction, pure and simple. One of those who saw it clearest was teammate Danny Frisella, who said, "The front office will make up his salary on one good weekend." Then the reliever added wistfully, "They can make up my salary with a rainout."

Off the field, Pete Rose might not quite qualify for a chair at Harvard—his ex-wife, Karolyn, claimed he had read only one book in his life, *The Life Story of Pete Rose*—but on the field Rose was as close to a genius as one can get. Take the time in 1976 at Wrigley Field. Standing in the batter's box, the Cincinnati spark plug, who had a habit of watching the ball all the way into the catcher's mitt, noticed that the ball had a black spot on it. Rose didn't say anything. On the next pitch, however, he yelled, "Hey, ump, that ball has a black spot on it." Both the Cub catcher and the umpire thought Rose had seen the black spot as the ball went by him. The umpire asked, "How the hell did you see that?" Rose answered, "Hey, I can see Chub Feeney's name on the ball when it comes in." Not only did Rose add to his already glowing reputation, his ploy helped destroy the pitcher's rhythm, allowing Rose to hit a rare home run on the next pitch.

Just when the normal bookkeeper's mind would have rebelled at the thought of all the heroics he had watched—including but hardly limited to, Bernie Carbo's tying home run, George Foster's perfect throw home to erase Denny Doyle at the plate with the potential winning run, Fred Lynn's collision with "the Wall," and Red Sox right fielder Dwight Evans's improbable leaping catch of Joe Morgan's probable homer—Cincinnati Reds star Pete Rose came to the plate in the extra innings of one of the greatest games ever played, the sixth game of the 1975 World Series. Looking down at Boston Red Sox catcher Carlton Fisk, who would later add one more chapter with his own game-winning homer, Rose said, "Geez, this is some game, isn't it?"

There have been television interviews and then again there have been television interviews. But there has never been an interview like the one Doug Rader once gave Jim Bouton. Here was Bouton, the pitcher-turned-sportscaster, resplendent in his ABC-TV blazer, pointing the microphone in the direction of the Houston third baseman, hoping to get Rader, in the words of ABC-TV, "up close and personal." What he got instead was a far-out Rader. Standing shirtless and leaning on a rake, his freckled cheek bulging with chewing tobacco and his red hair in what he called "Afro-barnyard" style, Rader stared at Bouton during his opening question: "How did you become a ballplayer?" Rader responded with a solemn, "On account of my environment. When you're always stealing hubcaps and doing time in jail, you can't help but become a ballplayer."

So much for that question, thought Bouton, hurrying right along to his next: Rader's advice for kids in the little leagues. "They should chew the gum that comes with baseball cards," Rader said, his freckled face not betraying the tongue wedged somewhere south of his cheekbone. "And then they should also eat the cards. Bubble-gum cards are very good in a little leaguer's diet," he went on. Bouton, now caught up in the game, threw in, *"Any* old bubble-gum cards?" "No," Rader answered quickly, "They should only eat the cards of the good ballplayers. You don't want them digesting bad statistics, which would hurt them. Say you got a kid who's five foot one. Let him eat a Willie McCovey card—Willie's six four. The kid may grow. You never can tell. . . ." And with that, Rader bit off a piece of a baseball card he had in his hand as Bouton dissolved in laughter and the ABC-TV image dissolved, period.

When Reggie Jackson first came to New York as a member of the Yankees, he boasted, "They'll name a candy bar after me." And, sure enough, Standard Brands named a candy bar "Reggie." Several of his teammates, however, insisted that the confectioners had wasted their money inasmuch as they already had a bar named after him: Butterfinger. On opening day, 1978, Standard Brands handed out the orange-wrapped bars, which had a Frisbee-like shape. And when Reggie hit a homer his first time at bat, the 50,000-plus in attendance scaled almost that many bars down on the field, making it, as writer Dick Schaap said, "the first time a game was ever delayed on account of candy bars."

By 1970 the phrase "It's easier to sneak a sunrise past a rooster than a ball past Hank Aaron" had become so much a part of baseball's fabric that it could have been woven into a sampler. Ron Klimkowski, a New York Yankee pitcher, was woefully aware of the cliché as he prepared to pitch to Aaron in a preseason exhibition game against Aaron's Atlanta Braves. Suddenly, the clouds opened up, and a thunderstorm washed the game out. Afterward, Yankee infielder Pete Ward came up to congratulate Klimkowski. "That's the best I've ever seen Aaron handled. When he came to bat, everyone walked off the field."

Everyone has one of those days: like Joe Torre had when, on July 21, 1975, he tied a major league record by grounding into four double plays. Each time the party of the second part was fellow Met Felix Milan, who had singled each time up just before Torre came to the plate. After the game Torre, tired of wearing the goat's horns, asked, "What's everyone blaming me for? Blame Felix. I wouldn't have hit into all those double plays if he hadn't hit all those singles."

Boston left-hander Bill Lee was known as "the Spaceman," a nickname that described the eccentric southpaw well. Lee, who wore number 37, opted for 337. Why, he was asked by some inquiring mind who wanted to know. "Because," said the lefty, standing up for his rights, "if you turn 337 upside down, it spells 'LEE.' And then I could stand on my head and people would know me right away."

To many, pitching is a case of mind over matter. Yankee reliever Ryne Duren, whose glasses looked like the ends of Coke bottles, tried to intimidate the batter—and often did, by throwing his first warm-up pitch over the catcher's head back to the screen. Others have psyched themselves to the point that they exclude everything but the enemy before them, trying to transmit a surliness and hate that transcends intimidation. One of those who practiced the latter theory of pitching was Goose Gossage. One time, as Gossage was standing on the mound, his Yankee hat pulled down over his eyes, his facial muscles tensing, his Fu Manchu mustache twitching, Yankee catcher Barry Foote came out to the mound to discuss something or other. His concentration momentarily broken, Gossage yelled at Foote to "get the hell back behind the plate." Foote, having none of it and obviously not on the same wavelength as Gossage, shouted back to his pitcher, "Go to hell yourself." And for more than ten seconds the two battery mates stood on the mound screaming epithets at one another before their "meeting" came to an end.

Baseball has had "fans" ever since Chris Von der Ahe, the owner of the old-old St. Louis Browns, devised the term, a contraction of the word "fanatics." Through most of baseball history some of the most vocal were those found in Ebbets Field, the "Dodger Faithful," who, egged on by a five-piece band wearing tattered clothing and playing something that resembled music through battered instruments—the beloved "Brooklyn Sym-Phony"—would make the afternoon or evening unbearable for Dodger opponents.

In recent years the "Bleacher Bums" who inhabit the left-field bleachers in Wrigley Field, Chicago, have matched the sound and fury of anything ever heard at Ebbets Field. And even raised it some. Arriving a full two hours before the start of every Cubbie afternoon game, the "Bums" begin cheering. Or singing such songs as "Mine Eyes Have Seen the Glory of the Coming of the Cubs" or old standards like "Give Me That Old-Time Durocher." Wearing blue hard-hats and T-shirts reading "Cub Fever—Catch It . . . and Die," or no shirts at all, their presence on any given afternoon is more than enough to make up for any deficiencies among their heroes on the field. One time they loosed seven white mice on the field to bedevil the visiting St. Louis Cardinals. On other occasions, they quickly—and scornfully—throw back onto the field all home-run balls hit into their sector by Cub opponents, complete with shouts of "We don't want it! We don't want it!" Any fan who succumbs to the traditional desire to keep the home-run memento is bombarded with chants from his neighbors: "Throw it back! Throw it back!" Their partisan rooting has so nettled Cubs' opponents that many a visiting player has been heard to mutter aloud, "Doesn't anybody in Chicago work in the afternoon?"

Prince Rainier of Monaco, better known as the husband of Grace Kelly, was on a grand tour of the United States when he found himself in the Astrodome, the indoor arena that bills itself as "the Eighth Wonder of the World," watching the inmates, the Houston Astros. Trying to make conversation, one of his hosts asked the Prince, "How would you like to have the Astrodome in Monaco?" To which the Prince answered, "Marvelous. Then we could be the world's only indoor country."

The roster of the Boston Red Sox in the early 1970s was peopled with several individualists who didn't quite subscribe to the prevailing New England conscience, which dictates that you can do anything but you can't enjoy it. They seemed to do everything and enjoyed every moment of it. Their resident zany was pitcher Bill "Spaceman" Lee, who, it was suggested, "not only threw lefthanded, but thought the same way." There were others, like outfielder Bernie Carbo, pitcher Rick Wise, pitcher Fergie Jenkins, and pitcher Luis Tiant, to name a few.

One of the least-recognized flakes on the team—for one short year, 1974—was pitcher Juan Marichal. Marichal was responsible for bringing an ever-increasing number of exotics into the clubhouse, including, one time, a Rumanian midget billed as "the World's Smallest Man." But the little Rumanian somehow disappeared, and the members of the team—many of whom thought a metronome was a midget who worked for MGM—fanned out in a search party to find him. Just when they were about to give up and call the Boston constabulary, the midget was finally located, asleep in an old catcher's mitt.

For one short year, 1976, Mark Fidrych lit up the baseball landscape. He talked to baseballs, tore up the pea-patch known familiarly as the pitcher's mound, and, not incidentally, won nineteen games for the Detroit Tigers. Along the way he also gained a nickname, "the Bird," and a reputation as a flake. Fidrych always claimed he was "not a flake" but couldn't prove it by his actions, one of which was to purposely spit tobacco juice all over the front of his shirt because, as he explained it, he "wanted the guys to know I chew."

Writer Roger Kahn and Brooklyn Dodger pitcher Carl Erskine became fast friends after Kahn's magnum opus, *The Boys of Summer*. On one occasion, while the two were making a stopover to publicize the book, Erskine began talking about the Fellowship of Christian Athletes. Kahn smiled at Erskine and allowed him to go on. But when Erskine brought up the Fellowship of Christian Athletes a second and then a third time, Kahn had had enough and interjected, "I'm thinking of starting a Fellowship of Jewish Athletes." Erskine arched his eyebrows ever so imperceptibly and allowed himself a "Who would be in that?" to escape from his lips. Kahn, now sure of his quarry, answered, "Koufax and Greenberg." "Oisk" looked at Kahn a second and then, with a touch of comical seriousness, said, "Not too numerous . . . but very gifted."

The
Eighties

Atlanta Braves pitcher Pascual Perez could usually locate the plate. But the ballpark was another matter. Scheduled to make his first start after being called up from the minors in 1982, Perez somehow got lost on his way to Fulton County Stadium. Three times he missed the exit off Highway I-285 leading to the stadium. After driving around the entire city of Atlanta four times without passing "Go" and without collecting $200, Perez found that he had to stop for gas. Then, finding he had no money, he had to borrow ten dollars from the station attendant to get back on the road. Presumably, he also got directions, because he finally arrived at the park—in the second inning. Braves manager Joe Torre took Perez's truancy in stride and made the most of the situation, giving Perez the number "I-285" to wear on the back of his warm-up jacket.

Manager Earl Weaver of the Baltimore Orioles was a five-foot-eight bantam rooster, a smoldering volcano in uniform who would do anything to make his point—throw equipment, kick his cap, put his finger in an umpire's face, cover home plate with dirt, or anything else among his medley of old favorites. His best tirade came in 1980, and it was worthy of both an Oscar and a three-day suspension. Weaver, more than somewhat displeased with either an umpire's ruling or the performance of his team—the cause of his outbreaks made little difference to Weaver and little sense to others—came barreling out to confront umpire Steve Palermo. After going through his entire repertoire, Weaver perched atop second base. Palermo, commenting later on his expulsion of the Oriole manager, said, "I guess Earl figures that's the only way he could be as tall as we are. But they don't make bags that tall."

Baseball announcers are with each other day after day for more than seven months a year, swapping stories, lies, and occasionally a baseball score or two. Sometimes their familiarity with one another breeds contempt. There was the time Phil Rizzuto and Fran Healy shared the Yankee broadcast booth. Or, to be more accurate, didn't share it, for Rizzuto had to excuse himself to honor a call of nature. On his return to the Yankee booth high atop Comiskey Park, he was greeted by his broadcast partner with a "Here's Scooter, back from the men's room." Rizzuto, who had heard it all during his long career with the Yankees, wasn't quite prepared for Healy's locker-room greeting and politely told his partner—and the millions listening—"Healy, you huckleberry, you're not supposed to tell people that. Tell them I went down to see Bill Veeck, the White Sox owner. And besides," continued Rizzuto, "I've been drinking coffee all day. And you know what happens when you drink coffee all day?" "No, what's that, Scooter?" asked Healy dutifully, setting up a straight line. "You go see Bill Veeck a lot."

The countdown was on. Pete Rose was only forty-seven hits shy of Ty Cobb's all-time hit total. And, without any deadline, timetable, or pressure, was moving inexorably toward the mark. Midway through the 1985 season Rose singled in his first at-bat against the Dodgers, bringing his total to 4,145. But then the rains came and the game was washed out, along with Rose's hit. All of which prompted one writer, John Strege, to write, "Ty Cobb, wherever he is, had a good day Wednesday. He actually gained on Pete Rose."

Mike Downey, writing in the Detroit Free Press, printed the following letter: "Q. If the Dodgers start an infield of Guerro, Anderson, Sax, and Brock, with Oliver in left field and Marshall in right, what advice do you have for their opponents?" Downey's answer: "Hit it fair."

Steve Sax, it was suggested by some wags, wears a glove on his left hand for much the same reason Michael Jackson does: for no apparent reason. Almost from the time Sax replaced the smooth-fielding Davey Lopes at second for the Los Angeles Dodgers, he began to give his best imitation of Ray Guy kicking the ball around the field. No amount of counseling by Sax's manager, Tommy Lasorda, worked. Finally, Lasorda—whose every move (before his recent weight loss) seems dictated by food, so much so that his own troops call him Tommy Lasagna—was moved to try another course. A main course, in fact. And so, one night after a game in Philadelphia, Sax returned to his hotel room to find the head of a pig with an apple in its mouth under the covers of his bed. Attached was a note, which read, "Play better baseball—or else, Signed, The Godfather." Sax took less time to figure out who did the dastardly deed than to read the note, remembering that roast pork had been a main course served earlier that day at a restaurant owned by Lasorda and his brothers.

Charlie Lau was reputed to be the greatest batting instructor this side of Ted Williams—even though he spotted "the Splendid Splinter" 2,300-plus hits and some 89 points in lifetime batting average. After his less-than-sterling career was over, Lau became the batting guru for several players, including George Brett. So when Brett got off to a slow start in 1985, he checked an instructional video on hitting made by Lau before his death the previous year. Brett went on a ten-for-twenty-four batting tear. "It was," he explained, "the first time I'd seen Charlie since the funeral."

Baseball players, unlike many of their fans, are rarely caught up in the mental underwear of comparisons or past history. Exhibit A toward this finding might well be Don Mattingly, the Yankee slugger who in his fourth year of play became the first Yankee with back-to-back forty-doubles seasons since Lou Gehrig had accomplished the feat some four decades earlier. When Mattingly was asked to make the inevitable comparison between himself and the "Iron Horse," he surprised many by answering, "To be honest, I had never heard of Gehrig until I came here. And, honestly, at one time I thought Babe Ruth was a cartoon character." In response to raised eyebrows he added, "I really did. I mean, I wasn't born until 1961." So much for history, which sportswriter "Bugs" Baer has called "petrified imagination."

In early 1987 Mickey Mantle suffered what was first thought to be a heart attack, but which, fortunately, turned out to be nothing more than a severe case of exhaustion. During the night in the hospital, Mantle said he had a dream. "I dreamt I died and went to heaven," Mickey remembered. "I'm waiting at the Pearly Gates and St. Peter asked who I was. I answered, 'Mickey Mantle.' And he said, 'Oh, good, God wants to talk to you.' So I go in and God says, 'Because of the life you led on earth we can't let you stay here. But before you go, would you sign these six dozen baseballs?'"

No one ever called Jay Johnstone normal. But the man who combined his last days in the majors as a designated hitter and a designated flake outdid himself when he was observed waiting in line at Chavez Ravine for a hot dog while the game was going on. In uniform.

New York Met rookie Kevin Mitchell came roaring into third base and turned to San Diego Padres third baseman Graig Nettles and said, "My dad says hello!" The surprised Nettles turned to Mitchell and said, "Who's your dad?" Mitchell, twenty-four years old, then told Nettles, forty-one, that his father, Earl Mitchell, had been a backcourt partner with Nettles on the San Diego High School basketball team of 1960–61. Nettles suddenly felt older.

The 1985 Giants, on their way to one of their worst seasons in the history of the hyphenated New York–San Francisco franchise, still tried to promote what little they had. And so it was that one afternoon at Candlestick Park the message board happily flashed a sign that read "Real Grass, Real Sunshine, Real Ball." Rocky Bridges, coach of the Giants, tried to put the slogan into perspective. "Well, two out of three ain't bad," said the resident pixie.

Ever since the lords of baseball abolished the spitball, the shineball, and other freak pitching deliveries, starting with the 1920 season, pitchers have tried to get around the prohibition. One such pitcher was Seattle Mariner Rick

Honeycutt, who in 1981 was caught illegally doctoring a baseball. Honeycutt was suspended for ten days and fined $500 for taping a thumbtack to his glove. Honeycutt, however, had been somewhat less than successful at his efforts. For not only was he caught red-handed, literally, but also, according to Honeycutt, "I only scuffed the ball on two pitches. And on those two, the Kansas City hitters got back-to-back singles. They complained that something was wrong with the ball. But they should have waited until I started getting somebody out."